If I Knew What Happened Next!

If I Knew What Happened Next!

Glyn Barrett

New Wine Press

New Wine Ministries
PO Box 17
Chichester
West Sussex
United Kingdom
PO19 2AW

ISBN 978-1-903725-98-6

Typeset by CRB Associates, Reepham, Norfolk
Cover design by CCD, www.ccdgroup.co.uk
Printed in Malta

Contents

Dedication

To Audacious City Church – great people, in a great city,
living out a great purpose for an extraordinary God

Acknowledgements

Sophia, Georgia and Jaedon. I love that I get to do life with you guys. You amaze me every day.

Mum and Sian. Thanks for all your love, patience and support!

Dave, Jen and Hope City Church. Thanks for the last eleven years. Your next decade will be incredible!

Tim – thanks for publishing and for the edit ... We made the deadline ☺

Hannah and Craig thanks for the typing!

Stuart and Dez, love you guys heaps.

Matt and Lyndsey, Foz and Em, Joel and Becky (thanks for the emails and SMSs), Jen. Wow, who was expecting this part of the journey?

The Audacious Band, Lindsey, Laney, Carlsberg, Deanna, Matt and Elena, Nate and Nikki, Naomi – absolute legends! What a ride!

Paul and Rachel in Youth Alive UK ... the future ... watch this space!

The guys at Planetshakers and Youth Alive Australia. You are a constant inspiration. If you can do it in the colonies, then we can do it in the home of the empire ☺

Jesus, I am constantly glad that YOU know what happens next. All for You!

Someone once said,

" 'Employee of the month' is a good example of how somebody can be both a winner and a loser at the same time."

Chapter 1

The part you HAVE to read

The other day, my friend sent me an SMS with the heading "women drivers!" I was intrigued. It read...

> Driving to the office this morning on the M62[1] motorway, I looked over to my right and there was a woman in a brand new BMW doing 90 miles per hour with her face up close to her rear view mirror putting on her eyeliner!

I couldn't believe what I was reading! "Are you serious?" I thought, lifting my eyes to the heavens in absolute amazement. "What was she thinking? Didn't she have any idea that she could kill someone doing that?" It continued,

> I looked away for a couple of seconds and when I looked back she was halfway over in my lane still working on that make-up! It scared me...

Yeah, it would scare me too! I couldn't believe what I was reading. I must admit though, as a driver I have seen a few crazy things in my time:

- Drivers using a PSP

- Drivers picking their nose (It's amazing how, when in a car, people settle into their own world, forgetting the fact that the people in the car next to them can clearly see them going at their nostrils! Yuk, I feel ill now.)
- Drivers singing at the top of their voice (especially hilarious when in stationary traffic and their sun roof is open, and they have forgotten that it is open, AND ... they can't sing a note in tune!)

But I have never seen a woman doing 90mph whilst applying make-up. This is madness, craziness, life endangeringness (I made that word up!) I continued reading...

> It scared me so much that I dropped my electric shaver, which knocked the bacon roll out of my other hand...

Ooooh, I get it now, it's a joke...

> In all the confusion of trying to straighten up the car using my knees against the steering wheel, it knocked my mobile from my ear, which fell into the coffee between my legs, causing it to splash and burn me, causing me to scream, which made me drop the cigarette out of my mouth, ruining my shirt and DISCONNECTING AN IMPORTANT CALL ... typical women drivers!

I am pretty sure that just like me, when you read the opening statement of that SMS, you were thinking, *"This madness, craziness, life endangeringness..."* and in the process you found yourself NEEDING TO KNOW ... (all together now) ... WHAT HAPPENED NEXT?

Imagine what life would be like if we all had the ability to know what happened next...

If I knew what was going to happen next, I wouldn't have made that bomb,[2] but I would have tied up those swimming shorts.[3] I would have videoed the "spaceship" moment,[4] but I would not have taken my wife to that game.[5] I know I definitely wouldn't have thrown that slipper at my sister, eaten in that particular restaurant that night, entered that posh museum in Paris with THAT particular friend (that's a whole other story for another time). And I am sure that I wouldn't have even got out of bed on that other particular day (more on that one later).

The fact is, if I knew what was going to happen next, I would have done a lot of things in life differently. I'm sure you are nodding as you read this, listing all the things you would have done differently if only you knew ... (all together now) ... WHAT HAPPENED NEXT?

What happened next in the Bible?

I love the Bible. It's exciting, dangerous, passionate, adventurous, mystical, fantastical (is that a word?), inspiring, weird, simple, confusing, relevant, irrelevant (can I say that?), majestic, private, friendly, X-rated ... yep, the Bible rocks! I remember my Dad telling me, *"Glyn, if there is ever anything you want to read about: adventure, passion, love ('Yuk dad, I'm only eight!'), spies, murder, sport,[6] war, disasters ... it's all in the Bible!"* Dad was right! The Bible is awesome. The stories are phenomenal. When you read it, imagine you are there. Use different voices for different characters. Mix it up a little. Don't give God a deep booming voice, give him a high-pitched one (I don't think that's sacrilegious), give Esther a deep voice and give the Apostle Paul a good London accent!

So the Bible is awesome, BUT ... it is also one of the most frustrating books in the world. Frustrating, because it doesn't always tell us WHAT HAPPENED NEXT!

Here are some examples and I hope that you too share my frustration with it:

1. In Genesis 11 we read about the Tower of Babel. At that time God confused the languages of mankind, but I want to know ... WHAT HAPPENED NEXT? Were families separated because they couldn't understand each other? Did Spanish start then? Did people speak Welsh, Aramaic and Italian, or did they cluck like chickens and bark like dogs? I don't know!!!

2. In 2 Kings 13:31 we read about the body of a dead man being thrown into the tomb of Elisha because a band of raiders was coming into town and the people wanted to get rid of the dead guy quick! When the dead guy's body touched the bones of Elisha the dead guy came back to life. Now I want to know ... (all together now) ... WHAT HAPPENED NEXT? Did the raiders kill him? (that would have been ironic). Did he walk home for fish and chips with his family? Did his family fall over when he walked through the front door? And while we are at it, why didn't Elisha come back to life?

3. In 2 Kings 6 we read about Elisha and his servant. They are surrounded by the enemy and the servant freaks out. Elisha is quite relaxed though, and after praying

that God would open the eyes of the servant, he sees the armies of heaven surrounding their enemies. I'll admit, it's a great story, but WHAT HAPPENED NEXT? Was the battle impressive? What did the armies of heaven look like? Did the servant get to watch the battle? And was the "Captain of the Hosts"[7] leading the armies of heaven? I wish I knew!

4. In Daniel 3 we read about Shadrach, Meshach and Abednego in the fiery furnace. We know that God saved them from the fire and that they got out of it, but WHAT HAPPENED NEXT? Did they start a fire walking troupe and travel around as entertainers? Did they die from natural causes or disease brought on through passive smoking? I don't know!

5. After Malachi 4:6 (page 883 in my Bible), there are four hundred years of silence before Jesus enters the world scene. After Malachi 4:6, WHAT HAPPENED NEXT? What happened in verse 7? I know there isn't a verse 7 and I am keenly aware I don't want to add to the pages of the Bible (see Revelation 22:18 – page 1153 in my Bible), but WHAT HAPPENED?

6. In Luke 2 shepherds appear at the birth of Jesus. Then WHAT HAPPENS? We don't hear about them again. Did they write books and become best-selling authors? Did they have trouble convincing their friends what they saw? *"Oh! You saw angels and heard them singing did you? Any pigs flying up there too?"*

7. What about the daughter of Herodius in Matthew 14? King Herod asked her to dance but she refused. The king offered her up to half the kingdom if she would dance and she still refused. Eventually Herodius convinced her daughter to dance for the king and as payment she

convinced her daughter to ask for the head of John the Baptist. Imagine the moment. She has danced and now she is back in her bedroom. She had the opportunity of wealth, fame and fortune, but instead she has the head of a dead man on her dressing table. Please, (all together now) ... WHAT HAPPENED NEXT? Was she happy about it? Did she stand in front of the mirror and shout "What was I thinking?" I don't know!

8. In Mark 2 we read about Jesus speaking in a house that was so jammed with people that the friends of a paralyzed man, in order to get him in front of Jesus, had to tear off the roof and lower him down, placing him on the floor in front of Jesus. We know that Jesus healed him, but ... WHAT HAPPENED NEXT? Who fixed the roof?

9. On the day Jesus died we read in Matthew 27:42 that, *"Holy men came alive"* WHAT HAPPENED NEXT? What happened when long dead husbands, fathers, uncles and brothers turned up on doorsteps saying, "Surprise!" How did they explain why they were there? Did they even know how it happened?

I don't know the answer to any of these questions because the Bible doesn't tell us WHAT HAPPENED NEXT!

Live in retrospect

It's a shame that we can't live our lives in "retrospect"! "What's that?" you say. The dictionary defines it as,

- Retrospect – ret·ro·spect – [re-truh-spekt] Looking back on or dealing with past events; with hindsight; *"Perhaps in retrospect, I shouldn't have gone."*

If you have heard anyone say, "If only I knew back then what I know now, I would have done something different." That is retrospect.

Overwhelming evidence proves to us that life is full of moments where if we knew what was going to happen "NEXT", we definitely would have done something different, so that our "NEXT" was different, because in the "NOW" we did something that changed what our "NEXT" actually was after the new "NOW" that we did before the new "NEXT". Confused? Me too, I'll see if I can explain it better.

We all live our lives based on NEXT! We buy food based on what we want to *eat* NEXT. We buy clothes based on what we want to *wear* NEXT. And we plan our holidays based on where we want to *visit* NEXT. It's not rocket science, it's just that we are always consciously or unconsciously planning our NEXT big thing. What we do NOW, determines what happens NEXT.

The genius of the day

There is one thing we can't factor into our planning, however, and that is the genius of the day.

God created the first day and it is an undeniable fact that God is amazing. Who else but God could have invented the brilliance of "a day"? It starts with breakfast ... bacon (God made pigs), eggs (God make chickens – but which came first, the chicken or the egg?), beans (God made ... err, dunno where beans come from!), sausages, black pudding, tomato sauce! (I'm feeling hungry after writing that!)

Then, you shower, shave perhaps, dress (not in a dress, unless you are a lady ...), apply make-up (again, if you are a lady, or alternatively you can try applying it whilst driving at 90mph with your face up to the rear view mirror[8]) and think about the day. However, the genius of the day is not breakfast (although God had a great idea with that), nor is it choosing what to wear from your wardrobe (obviously, don't wear your wardrobe ... it's a bit stiff). The genius of the day is that *you are never quite sure what is going to happen next!* You plan one thing and something completely different takes place. NB: You'll love "the day from hell" in this book. I will tell you about something bizarre that took place in my life one day, but I won't tell you what happens next until the next chapter – get it? "If I knew what happened next!" – you'll have to read the next chapter to find out what happened next, but if you stop reading this after three chapters like some of those other books on your bookshelf, then you will never know what happened next on that fateful day. And, after all, we all want to know ... (all together now) ... "WHAT HAPPENED NEXT?"

Coming up:

"Aaaaaaachooooo!"

Notes

1. The M62 is a motorway in England that runs from Kingston upon Hull to Liverpool. The journey will take you about two and a half hours – unless you drive near a lady doing 90mph whilst applying make-up. You may never reach your destination!
2. See *If I Was the Devil*, the first book in this series!
3. Ibid (meaning same as the footnote above).
4. See *If I Had a Face Like Yours*, the second book in this series!
5. Ibid.
6. Joke: What is the first recorded sport in the Bible? Tennis! Because Joseph served in Pharaoh's court! Yep, it's bad, that's why it's an endnote and not up there in the big writing area!
7. The "Captain of the hosts" is a title given to Jesus Christ. It would have been cool to watch Jesus take on the enemy.
8. This author does not condone such behaviour. I was merely referring to the opening story in the book and will not be held responsible for such madness, craziness, and life endangeringness.

Chapter 2

The part you REALLY HAVE to read

Let's face the facts for a moment. If I knew what was going to happen next, five things would happen to me. (Don't think you can read these next five points and know what the rest of the book will say. Not true. These points are added extras.)

▶ *1. I'd make a killing*
Everyone in society is looking for assurance for the next phase of life. That's why people have guarantees and warrantees, savings and pensions, life insurance and wills, TV guides and horoscopes.

Tarot card readers make a mini-fortune "predicting" people's futures. Imagine how much money I could make if I *definitely* KNEW WHAT HAPPENED NEXT in people's lives. People would pay me big money to know things like when they were going to die, who they would marry, what job they should take. Not to mention the fact that I would win the lottery every weekend, because I KNEW WHAT HAPPENED NEXT.

▶ *2. Life would be dull!*
Can you imagine walking home from school and as you

come through the front door your family shout, "Surprise!" and you reply, "I knew it!"

Life would be boring. No surprise parties, no excitement about presents (you know what's under the wrapping), no WOW moment when you meet the person of your dreams for the first time, because you knew what would happen next!

▶ *3. Life would be scary*

Imagine knowing the exact moment you are going to get sick. The time is 3:46:04 ... 5 seconds, 6, 7 ... "AHCHOOOOOOO!!!". "Yep, I sneezed at exactly 3:46pm and 7 seconds as expected!"

Or, even more bizarrely, imagine knowing the exact moment you are going to die. That is too freaky to even think about. What do you do in the seconds, minutes and hours leading up to that moment? It's bad enough knowing what time you are going to have a dentist appointment! Perhaps though, if you knew exactly when you were going to die, you would do something different NOW, which may change your NEXT so that maybe you don't die after all? It's all very confusing.

▶ *4. I wouldn't need to rely on God!*

I suppose if I knew what happened next I wouldn't have to rely on God as much. I could just work things out and change them before they happened. The fact that I don't know what happens next means that I am compelled to pray and ask God for His help and guidance!

▶ *5. I'd be God*

In a strange way, if I knew what happened next, I would be God! In Acts 1:7 Jesus says, *"It is not for you to know the*

times or dates the Father has set by his own authority...
And so I suppose, knowing what will happen next is
something only God can know. God is awesome though.
Sometimes He gives us windows into what the future holds,
that's called prophecy, or even words of wisdom.

It is clear that we can never fully know what's going to
happen next. (The genius of the day will take care of that.)
There is one thing we can do however. We can do our best to
"set up" our NEXT as much as possible, so that perhaps our
NEXT will be ok.

Nature teaches us the principle that the farmer sows his
seed into the field NOW, knowing that when the NEXT
harvest time comes, he will have a crop to harvest.

The Bible says that in life you "reap what you sow" (see
2 Corinthians 9:6). So in your NOW, if you do the right
things – invest your time, energy, actions and even finances
well – then you are setting up your NEXT to be a success.

If much of what happens NEXT is determined by what
you do NOW (the genius of the day excluded), what sort of
things should you KNOW and what sort of things should you
DO in the NOW to set up your NEXT as an opportunity to
live an exciting life?

The rest of this book is devoted to that very thing!

Grab your Bible and a drink. You are going to love this!

Coming up:

"The day from hell!"

Someone once said,

"I spent a year in that church,
one Sunday."

Chapter 3

The day from hell!

April 12th 1990[1]

Dear Diary,

Why me? I am an average, ordinary, down to earth guy. I got yelled at; I was embarrassed, I nearly killed myself, the geese attacked me again, I ruined that dude's clothes AND I was lucky there was no car behind me. I didn't need that chemical solution and, worst still, I've got to go back and face the music tomorrow. Dad won't let me quit, Mum smiled and I'm sure I have got a nervous twitch that will make me the laughing stock of all the girls.

Here's what happened…

6:20am: Got out of bed and got dressed.

6:28am: Had some toast (with vegemite).

6:35am: Set off for work. Walking (can't wait to get a car!)

6:50am: Stopped to pick up Gaz at his house.

7:10am: Stopped at McDonalds and grabbed a hot chocolate.

7:30am: Arrived at work.

7:33am: Got chased by the "guard geese" again.[2]

7:34am: Drank a brew with Gaz and Pat, whilst plotting the demise of those geese.

7:45am: Said "G'day" to Boss and was given jobs for the day. (Pat and I have been fixing the front of a hairdressing salon that a bus had crashed into.)

7:48am: Got chased by the "guard geese" again. The Boss laughed.

7:50am: Drank a brew with Gaz and Pat, whilst plotting the demise of those geese.

7:58am: Loaded up the van with Pat and set off to the hairdressers (only about a mile away.)

8:05am: Arrived at hairdressers. The hairdresser made us a brew. We drank it whilst discussing, football, girls, food and the demise of those geese!

8:20am: Started the job and all hell broke loose! Why me?!

Coming up:
"The weird nose"

Notes

1. This is a true account of a day in my life. I was eighteen years old, working as a builder's labourer, saving money before going to Bible College.
2. The builder's yard kept getting broken into by thieves. The boss bought some ferocious geese to scare off would-be thieves at night. The trouble is the geese liked the thieves (they probably brought food) and hated us!

Someone once said,

"Before you criticize someone, you should walk a mile in their shoes. That way, when you criticize them, you're a mile away and you have their shoes."

Someone once said,

"I am nobody ...
nobody is perfect ...
I must be perfect then."

Next #1

If I knew what happened next, I would …

… not have gone to work that day

8:20am: Started the job and all hell broke loose! Why me?!

*I can't even think where it all went wrong! I suppose there was a whole list of things I could have done differently, but how was I supposed to know that all those things were going to happen one after the other? At one point I remember thinking to myself, "This sort of thing doesn't even happen in a well-scripted Mr Bean sketch! Why the heck did it happen to me today and WHY did I happen to be there at that moment? I suppose that if I knew what was going to happen next, I would have definitely done things differently. To be honest, if I knew all that was going to happen, I wouldn't have even gone to work today. Perhaps that's the answer. I should have just gone back to the starting point and **not** started … yeah … I might stay in bed tomorrow!*

Learning to re-define your starting point

I thought the answer was to go back to the beginning and either start again or, preferably, not start at all. It was my attempt at rectifying the situation. In reality the solution to my problem *was* back at the beginning of my nightmare day – just not in the way I thought. In life, often all we need to do is *re-define* our starting point and in doing so we realize that TODAY, NOW, is not as bad as we thought it was. A runner will tell you that races are often won and lost right at the starting line. In the Bible Paul tells us that life is like a race (see 1 Corinthians 9). We have got to understand and re-define our starting point and realize that what we are going through now in our life is part of a much bigger picture.

Is God at war?

I was recently praying about a situation, asking God to "have the victory" over it. I remember hearing God say to me, "I thought I did have the victory!" and I was instantly reminded of what Jesus said on the cross before He died. He said, *"It is finished!"*

It got me thinking. What exactly was "finished"? A lot of things: His mission to save man from the penalty and presence of sin; the curse of sickness and disease; lots of other hot issues you may have heard preached about in church etc.

But the statement "It is finished" covers more than that! In Ephesians 6:10–12 we read that there is battle going on in the *"heavenly realms"*. It is a spiritual battle and we assume that God is at war, that God is fighting the devil, that He is struggling with the enemy!

In the Old Testament, God is often presented as a battling, war-like God!

"The LORD will fight for you; you need only to be still!"
(Exodus 14:14)

"The LORD was fighting for Israel..."   (Joshua 10:14)

"The battle is the LORD's..."   (1 Samuel 17:47)

*"Who is this King of glory?...
    the LORD mighty in battle"*   (Psalm 24:8)

"The LORD will go out and fight..."   (Zechariah 14:3)

We have a picture of God that conjures up images of Braveheart, Alexander the Great or Lord Nelson. But something happened in the New Testament. There is a massive difference between Elijah, David, Samson, Gideon and you and me. That difference is ... God came to earth and declared, *"It is finished!"* In other words, not only is salvation assured for those who believe, but also, the battle is over; the war is won and victory in life is assured!

This may seem a little contentious, but I am not convinced that God is still fighting the devil! I am not sure He is struggling with the enemy or that He is in fact at war. *We* struggle, *we* fight, *we* are at war with the devil, but God has already won![1] God won at Calvary and two thousand years later we are just playing catch-up with that victory. Our "starting point" then, is not one of struggling and striving, but of victory. What we need to do is to take hold of it.

Listen to what Philippians 3:12–14 says:

> *"Not that I have already obtained all this, or have
> already been made perfect, but I press on to take hold of*

*that for which Christ Jesus took hold of me ... one thing
I do: Forgetting what is behind and straining toward
what is ahead, I press on toward the goal to win the
prize for which God has called me heavenward in
Christ Jesus."*

Look at the key words in these verses:

- press on
- take hold
- Jesus *already* took hold of me
- strain toward
- press on towards the goal
- win the prize

God's work with us is mostly His encouraging us to catch up
with the victory He accomplished on the cross. We have to
press on, strain towards, press on towards ... doesn't sound
easy does it?

A moment at the Olympics

I remember once watching a race in the Olympics. All the
runners had spent years preparing for it and it all came
down to the next nine seconds. Years of sacrifice, time and
energy had gone into this moment. This is what their life
was all about. As the starting gun sounded the athletes shot
out of their blocks just like bullets from a gun. One, two,
three seconds gone. One of the runners had emerged from

the blocks with a slight stumble which caused him to fall after three to four seconds. Within moments the crowd's gasps for the fallen athlete had merged into cheers as they applauded the victor of the race. How did the fallen runner feel at that moment? I would imagine he had mixed emotions, but the overriding emotion must have been one of disappointment, of regret and the sense of "why me?" I'll never forget the next few moments as they unfolded. The winner turned around and saw the fallen athlete. He jogged back to the runner on the floor, helped him to his feet, and together they jogged the final paces to the finish line. The crowd exploded with cheers for the victor AND the fallen athlete who had the courage to finish the race.

I think this best describes what God does for us. When He declared, *"It is finished,"* He was breaking the tape at the finish line. He won! And yet, He turns around and helps us. He encourages us when we need it and He helps us (if we take His offer of help) to the finish line! BUT, we have got to *press on, strain towards, press on towards the prize.*

Because of what Jesus accomplished on the cross and because Paul tells us that Christ has already taken hold of us, we can now understand a few things about our starting point in life. This is what is true about you:

1. You're not a nobody striving to become somebody. Jesus' death proved that you were a somebody who was important enough for Him to lay down His life for.
2. You're not a struggler striving to find breakthrough in life.
3. You're a victor coming to terms with what victory means for you.

The weird nose

The Bible says that you are "more than a conqueror" (see Romans 8:37) Have you ever stopped to consider what that actually means? In the city of Manchester where I live we have a world champion boxer. He trains, he gets in the ring and he wins. He wins plaudits, prize money, cars, watches, sponsorships and free clothes! If you were to look at him you would realize he is a boxer. Usually the nose is a telltale sign of a boxer. (Incidentally, at school, never pick a fight with a guy with a weird nose. He was either born with a weird nose or worse, he is a boxer. Stay away from weird nose people!)[2] He carries the scars of battle. He is a conqueror, but he's not "*more than* a conqueror". The "more than a conqueror" in this scenario is his wife. She doesn't get in the ring. She doesn't fight. She doesn't have a weird nose. She is beautiful. She wears designer clothing, drives posh cars and spends money as she sees fit. SHE is more than a conqueror. She is living off what the conqueror achieves in the ring! Likewise, Jesus is the conqueror. He has the scars of battle in His nail-scarred hands, the hole in His side and the whipped back. The Bible says that the Church is the "Bride of Christ". In other words, YOU are more than a conqueror!

What Jesus accomplished on the cross was projected into the future – projected all the way to the beginning of your life. You start at a place of victory. *"It is finished"* were victory words for you. Your life is signed, sealed and delivered in victory – you just have to catch up with what Jesus did for you!

Mindsets determine success and failure

I have discovered that the mindset with which I start a task often determines what the outcome will be.

When I was eighteen I started driving. I took four driving lessons and then took my driving test. My dad had said that all the examiners were looking for was confidence, so I thought to myself, "I can do confident!"

The day of the test arrived. It was at 5:00pm in Manchester (UK) and, yep, you guessed it, it was raining. I waited patiently (nervously actually) in the car for the examiner to approach me. As he started walking in my direction I jumped out of the car, shook his hand and introduced myself (consciously determining not to be arrogant or cocky). We circled the car as he checked its road-worthiness and then he sat in the passenger seat. As I click-clacked my seatbelt, I asked him if he had his belt on too, to which he nodded. But then he looked at me in disbelief when I asked if we could listen to the radio while I drove! "Perhaps I went too far?" I thought. He declined the offer of music in the car, citing that it may make it difficult for me to hear his instructions clearly (how loud did he think I was going to have it?).

5:00pm proved to be a great time to take my driving test. The test took forty-five minutes, but because of rush hour traffic, we only actually drove for about fifteen minutes of that time. I used the stationary moments as an opportunity to politely comment on other driver's mistakes in front of and beside us, to which the examiner agreed, and then we discussed football. At the end of the test he smiled and congratulated me on my "most excellent" driving skills and passed me. Very cool!

When I was twenty I moved to Sydney, Australia. I entered the licensing office to change my British driving licence into an Australian one. Imagine my horror when I discovered that they did not accept British licences! I would have to re-apply and re-do the theory and practical exams in order to get a driving licence. I was indignant! Didn't they realize I was British? Didn't they realize that the only reason Australia exists is because *we* settled it? (I understand this is a highly politically incorrect statement and probably not true – but I was indignant!) Didn't they realize they were still part of the British Empire? Didn't they realize they still had the Queen of England on their money? The only reason they had cars was because we invented them (or was it the Americans? Or the Germans? Let's just say it was the British, it makes me feel better – I was indignant!).

In disgust I re-applied and was given the date of my driving exam. I went into the licensing office again the day before the exam to confirm the time of the test. The lady assured me it was at 11:00am and that my driving examiner was standing on the other side of the office reception even as we spoke. (I remembered the words of my dad, "All the examiners are looking for is confidence . . .") I thanked the lady behind the counter and approached the examiner. Upon introduction, I heard the angelic tones of a lady speaking English with an English accent. I knew then the licence was signed, sealed and delivered – she was English!

The next day I arrived for my test dressed in a full England soccer kit! The examiner asked me where I was from. She said she was from Liverpool and during the whole test we talked about the differences between England and

Australia. At one point I brought up the subject of Australia not accepting English driving licences. She agreed that it was absurd! She continued, "Don't they realize we are British? Don't they realize that the only reason Australia exists is because we settled it? (She understood this was a highly politically incorrect statement and probably not true – but she was indignant!) Don't they realize they are still part of the British Empire? Don't they realize they still have the Queen of England on their money? The only reason they have cars is because we invented them!" (or was it the Americans? Or the Germans? Let's just say it was the British, it made her feel better – she was indignant!).

Needless to say ... I passed!

As I write this chapter, England stands in awe at a particular young footballer who last night scored some amazing goals for his team in the Champions League in Europe. Commentators have said he is the best in the nation, possibly the world. Others have agreed, saying there are other footballers with the same skill level, however this one player exudes the *confidence* that determines that every time he steps onto the field HE WILL score!

Mindset determines outcome!

Imagine if you approached life with a mindset that said, "I'm already victorious!" What would happen?

Finishing off the first Next now – so I can get onto what happened next...

Look at Philippians 3:12 again,

> *"Not that I have already obtained this or have been made perfect BUT . . . I press on to take hold of that for which* **Christ Jesus** [already] *took hold of me . . ."*
>
> (emphasis added)

I have often heard preachers refer to God's calling of Moses by quoting what God said to him: "What do you have in your hand?" (see Exodus chapter 3). From that basis they argue that life is all about what we have in our hand. What can we do? What skills do we have? Who do we know? What qualifications do we have? etc. However, your starting point in life (and this is the *re-defining* of your starting point) is not what you have in your hand, it is what God has in *His* hand. Philippians 3:12 says that Christ Jesus has already taken hold of us! Our starting point is that we are already in the palm of God's hand!

Your life is primarily not about what you have in your hand, but it is what God has in His hand . . . and He has you! That's how you can know everything will work out okay in the end!

I married the best girl in the world! On the day of the wedding I woke up and casually thought, "What's happening today?" Then it dawned on me. "Oh yeah, I'm getting married!" My best mate Lee ran into my room and jumped on me. After a few poundings I got up and together with the rest of my bridal party we washed the cars, ate McDonalds for breakfast and then played football in a park.

Sophia and I had decided to get married at 9:30am, thus beating the heat of the Australian sun. At 9:00am Lee shouted out, "Strewth, it's 9:00am and we gotta get ready!"

We jumped in the cars, raced back to the hotel. All four guys managed to get showered, dressed and to the church within twenty-five minutes arriving at 9:25am (only guys can do that!). At 9:30am, I turned to my best man and said, "Mate, have you got the rings?" to which he replied, "Holy cow, I left them in the hotel!" The boys laughed. I sighed a deep sigh that said, "God, why must I endure life with a bunch of friends who are moronic at best and bandits at worst!" One of the guys raced off in a flurry of smoking tyres and a screaming engine. Thankfully, Sophia was twenty-five minutes late (a habit she has yet to break ☺) and the rings arrived at the church before my wife-to-be. Phew, that was a close call!

Imagine if one of the guys had said, "Yeah, I know Lee forgot the rings, but I saw them on the table as we were leaving, so I picked them up. Here they are ... " as he produced them from his jacket pocket. That would have been a cool moment!

Over the years I have met many people who feel like they have wasted times and seasons in their lives. It's very much like the "ring moment" as they realize, "Oh no, I have forgotten to really live my life to the best and make the most of every moment." People look back with regret at wasted moments and missed opportunities. But it is at that moment that the BEST MAN, Jesus Christ, steps forward and says, "It's okay, I have your life in My hand right here, right now. If you are ready to really start living, then I'm here for you!" *Christ Jesus has already taken hold of you.* Your starting point is that you are in the palm of God's hand. You don't start from the place of defeat, but from the place of victory, where Jesus said, *"It is finished."*

Coming up:

"The Paddleboat Race!"

Notes

1. This is what theologians call "tension" or the "now – not yet". An example of theological tension includes, "We are saved from the penalty of sin, but will be saved from the presence of sin one day. We are saved and we will be saved. OR, the NOW of being saved but the NOT YET of being saved from the presence of sin in the future."

2. I am sorry if your nose is stranger than most. No offence is intended, this is just an attempt by me to break up the intensity of the moment by using some light humour directed at ... um ... your nose! Maybe I shouldn't put that paragraph in the book. If you are reading this right now, it is because my editor and publisher okayed it (blame Tim!).

Making it real for you!

1. Why do you think you may need to re-define your starting point?

   ....

   ....

   ....

2. What does the phrase "It is finished" mean for you in your world?

   ....

   ....

   ....

   ....

3. How will changing your mindset affect the way you live your life?

   ....

   ....

   ....

   ....

4. How does knowing that Jesus has you "already" in His hand help you?

   ....

   ....

   ....

   ....

Someone once said,

"Face it, ALL true wisdom
is found on T-shirts."

Next #2

If I knew what happened next, I would...

...not have put that stick there

8:20am: Started the job and all hell broke loose! Why me?

8:22am: Had a brew with Pat and the hairdresser. Hairdresser made insulting comments about our hair. I decided to add him to the list after the geese!

8:25am: The boss turned up and asked me to stand on the opposite side of the road to the hairdressers. He called across, "What can you see?" I replied, "A hairdressers!" The look of death he gave me made me realize he was serious. I looked back towards the hairdressers, admiring the new shop window we had put in place. Yep – that looked good. Admired the new door and all the brickwork. Couldn't see anything amiss until the boss pointed to a brick that was upside-down. I readily agreed with him (not actually realizing that you could have an upside-down brick). He told me to chisel it out, place a new one in and then paint all the bricks with magnolia coloured masonry paint.

8:27am: Removed one of the two sets of ladders from the roof of the van.

8:28am: Positioned the ladder against the front of the hairdressers.

8:29am: Grabbed the hammer and chisel and climbed the ladder. I was about to hit a brick when my boss yelled, "Not that one you idiot! Further up!" Locating the correct brick (or incorrect brick, whichever way you look at it), I proceeded to chip it out of the wall.

8:40am: Removed the rubble of the brick and cleared a space for the new brick.

8:44am: Mixed some mortar and located a new brick.

8:48am: Placed mortar and inserted brick. Pointed the edges of the brick.

8:52am: Drank a brew with Pat whilst admiring the new brick. Pat agreed that I was "an excellent bricklayer".

9:01am: Located the five-litre tub of magnolia masonry paint in the van. Opened the lid and stirred the paint. Found a stick, grabbed the paint and brush and climbed the ladder, ready to commence painting the front of the hairdressers.

9:03am: Inserted the stick into a hole on the top of ladders and hung the paint tub from the protruding stick. Checked to make sure said stick was able to carry the weight of a five-litre tub of paint and commenced painting.

9:09am: Painting went according to plan. Realized I needed a brew when all of a sudden I heard someone yell out, "Hey, is that you up the ladder, Glyn?"

Little did I know that THIS was to be my fatal error in judgment! Why did I stop and look down? Why did I put that stick in that hole? Why didn't I think, think, think?

A story about lettuce

A lady asked a man working in the fruit and vegetable department of a supermarket if she could buy half-a-head of lettuce. He replied, "Half-a-head? Are you serious? We only sell them as a full head!"

"You mean to tell me," she persisted, "that after all the years I've shopped here, you won't sell me half-a-head of lettuce?"

"Look," he said, "if you like I'll ask the manager."

She indicated that it would be appreciated, so the young man marched to the front of the store. "You won't believe this," he said to the manager, "but there's a lame-brained idiot of a woman back there who wants to know if she can buy half-a-head of lettuce." He noticed the manager gesturing and turned around to see the lady standing behind him, obviously having followed him to the front of the store. "And this nice lady here was wondering if she could buy the other half!" he concluded.

Later in the day the manager cornered the young man and said, "That was the finest example of thinking on your feet I've ever seen! Where did you learn that?"

The lad said, "I grew up in London and Londoners are renowned for their quick thinking. Incidentally, if you know anything about London, you'll know that it's also famous for its great football teams and its ugly women!"

The manager's face flushed. "My wife is from London!" he scowled.

"Really?" replied the young lad. "What club does she play for?"

How's that for quick thinking? I wish that when I first climbed that ladder I had given some thought to what I was doing and what could potentially happen if it went wrong.

One of the greatest challenges we face in life is to THINK about what we are doing and consider what will be the outcome of our actions.

The snake talks?

In Genesis 3 we read about an amazing discussion between Eve and a snake. If it is not amazing enough that she is talking to a snake, the topic of conversation is even more amazing. The snake (the Devil) says to Eve, *"God knows that when you eat* [the fruit] *your eyes will be opened, and **you will be like God**, knowing good and evil"* (verse 5, emphasis added). Eve then eats the fruit that God has forbidden (Adam eats too), and sin enters the world causing misery, pain, death and sorrow. Imagine if Eve had thought the whole thing through for a moment. Imagine if she would have thought about what God had said: *"Let us make man in our image..."* (Genesis 1:26). Adam and Eve were already like God and yet when the pressure was on, Eve didn't think! Now, because of her (and his) thoughtlessness, we live with the consequence of those actions.

Think about what you know and why

1 Peter 3:15 says,

> *"**Always be prepared to give an answer** to everyone who asks you to give the reason for the hope that you have."*
> (emphasis added)

It is amazing how many people believe what they believe because someone told it to them, therefore making it true!

As a child, my best mate would tell me stories that stretched the truth beyond all comprehension. For example, the time that NASA found a red double-decker London bus on the moon. I was amazed! How did they get a bus on the moon? I would run inside and tell my Mum these things to which she would ALWAYS reply, "Who told you that? Lee?" And yep, it always was.

In my theology lectures students say the most bizarre things. Usually they believe it because someone once told it to them. "Jesus is not God!" one of my students declared in class once. She didn't actually believe what she had said, she was just repeating something she'd heard and she wasn't thinking about it.

Much of our belief system comes from other people's convictions, rather than our own. We accept what others tell us rather than thinking things through. 1 Peter 3:15 teaches us the importance of THINKING! The story of Adam and Eve is teaching us the need to THINK! My day from hell as it unfolds over the next few chapters is teaching us the need to THINK about what we do before we do it!

Let me suggest two things worth thinking about and getting right. These will help your NOW to set up your NEXT!

1. Remember it's just "stuff!"

In my house we have a drawer. This drawer is the infamous "stuff" drawer! Recently, I pulled out the entire stuff drawer to see what was actually in there (yep, it was a real low moment in my life – I needed something to do!). In the drawer was:

- Spare keys to the house, the car, our luggage locks.
- New AND old batteries
- Take-a-way menus (that's where they were!)
- A sock!
- My dentist appointment card!

- Several random miscellaneous buttons of all colours and sizes
- A TV remote control
- Chewing gum (unchewed)
- Half a packet of mints
- Eyeliner pencils
- Blue-Tak
- Glue
- Pens (most didn't work)
- A needle and thread
- Postcards
- Random telephone numbers
- A Valentine's Day card
- One earring
- An important letter from my daughter's school requiring an immediate reply
- Plus other random bits and pieces that could fill this entire book!

I must admit, the drawer is a bit of a step down from what we had in our last house. We used to have a cupboard under the stairs that we nicknamed "hell!" No one ever wanted to go in there because you were likely to encounter Jason, Damien, the hockey mask dude, or worse still ... spiders! The trouble is, every miscellaneous item we had ended up in hell (under the stairs). Once a year I would clean it out, but then Jason, Damien, the hockey mask dude, and the spiders would gather more stuff in there including, toys, bags, shoes etc.

Our "stuff" drawer (just like hell) has a life of its own. It breeds and grows and will only ever be cleaned out when it can no longer close!

I know that as you are reading this, you too are thinking

about that drawer, cupboard, garage, room, attic, basement or shed your family has that is full of random, miscellaneous items. You too, if you are looking for something, probably realize it is in that location, but you are loathe to approach it because you too are fearful of Jason, Damien, the hockey mask dude, or worse still ... spiders!

Some people go one step further. They hire space in a warehouse for extra storage space. People actually pay money to store their stuff! It then becomes a vicious cycle:

- People get married and buy a house
- They end up with too much stuff and now need to buy a bigger house
- Now the bigger house has not enough stuff (it's a bit empty), so they buy more stuff for the house

And life becomes an endless quest to get stuff.

"Stuffed!"

My stuff drawer is "crammed" with stuff! Matthew 6:19–21 says,

> *"Do not store up for yourselves treasures on earth, where moth and rust destroy, and where thieves break in and steal. But store up for yourselves treasures in heaven, where moth and rust do not destroy, and where thieves do not break in and steal. For where your treasure is, there your heart will be also."*

Society is transfixed with the desire to have more stuff! Better this and more of that. Inevitably our stuff ends up in a drawer, garage, shed, attic, basement etc., and the things that were once so important are now relegated to the land of Jason, Damien, the hockey mask dude, and worse still ... spiders!

Ever looked at something you own and thought, "Why did I buy that?" and yet it seemed so important at the time! It's just stuff and life gets crammed with it!

In Matthew 6 Jesus is not saying "don't have stuff", but He is saying, "don't store it!" In other words don't let your purpose in life revolve around stuff! He didn't die on the cross for you to have lots of stuff and become consumed by acquiring of more and more of it. He died so that you could live out your destiny and enjoy a life of value and purpose.

You have to make the choice not to let "stuff" be the thing that dictates the way you will live! Otherwise, your life will just get stuffed and you will become like that space that belongs to Jason, Damien, the hockey mask dude, and worse still ... spiders. No one will want to go near you!

2. Make sure your NOW focuses on forever

Jesus says, "... *store up for yourselves treasures in heaven ...* ". In other words, Jesus says, "Think mostly about your NOW so that you have a great NEXT!"

When Mark married Emily

Mark met Emily and they fell in love! After several years of dating, Mark plucked up the courage to ask Emily to marry him. She gushed with emotion and said yes.

There is a part in the Marriage Vows that reads as follows,

- I "**Mark Jonathon Foster**"[1] take you "**Emily Victoria Cocker**"[2] to be my wife, to have and to hold from this day forward, for better or for worse, for richer, for poorer, in sickness and in health, to love and to cherish, from this day forward **until death do us part**.

Every day of marriage needs be about "until death do us part". In other words, forever!

- If you have a disagreement: Your "now" needs to focus on forever – until death do us part.
- If love goes cold: Your "now" needs to focus on forever – until death do us part.
- Affairs happen because the NOW focused only on the feelings of now and the forever part (until death do us part) was forgotten.

Many marriages have become "until I find a better option", or "until STUFF gets in the way" instead of "until death do us part".

The Paddleboat Race

There were two paddleboats. They left Memphis at about the same time, travelling down the Mississippi River to New Orleans. As they travelled side-by-side, some of the crew of one of the vessels made a few remarks about the snail's pace of the other.

Challenges were soon returned by the crew of the other boat and a race began. The competition became vicious as the two boats roared through the Deep South.

One boat began falling behind. There had been plenty of coal for a leisurely trip, but not for a race. As the boat dropped back an enterprising young sailor took some of the ship's cargo and tossed it into the furnace. When his crewmates saw that the supplies burned as well as the coal, they fuelled their boat with all the material they had been assigned to transport. They ended up winning the race, but burned their cargo![3]

God has entrusted a cargo to us, too: children, spouses, friends. Our job is to do our part in seeing that this cargo reaches its destination. Yet when "stuff" and "now" takes priority over "people" and "forever", we often end up sacrificing our "cargo" in order to get more stuff and live for now. We forget to focus on forever! Don't burn your cargo in order to reach your destination. Remember forever and live like that now!

Finishing off the second Next now – so I can get onto what happened next

It's worth taking the time to stop and think about things. Think about what is important; think about who is important to you; think about how you are living your life; think about what you are filling your life with and whether or not your NOW focuses on forever!

My maths teacher once insulted me by saying, "If you had

two brain cells Barrett, one of them would be lonely!" He was rudely teaching me the importance of THINKING!

It's worth taking the time to know what you believe about God.

If you remember not to be consumed by "stuff" and that you should focus on forever then you are setting yourself up for a great NEXT!

Coming up:

"Is God taking a leak?"

Notes

1. Fictional character.
2. So is this!
3. Max Lucado, *In the Eye of the Storm*, Word Publishing, 1991, pp. 97–98.

Making it real for you!

1. What do you think about the way you think?

   ....

   ....

2. Do you think your life is stuff-orientated?

   ....

   ....

3. How will having a "forever" mindset affect the way you live?

   ....

   ....

4. Think, what is important to you?

   ....

   ....

   ....

5. Think, who is important to you?

   ....

   ....

   ....

6. Think, what do you fill your life with?

   ....

   ....

   ....

Someone once said,

"Never trust a man who,
when left alone in a room with
a tea cozy, doesn't try it on."

Next #3

If I knew what happened next, I would . . .

. . . not have stopped to talk to that geezer

9:09am: Painting went according to plan. Realized I needed a brew when all of a sudden I heard someone yell out, "Hey, is that you up the ladder, Glyn?" I looked down and saw Mike an old friend of mine who was a painter and decorator. "G'day," I said, "fancy a brew?"

9:14am: Sat down for a cup of tea and chatted with my buddy, who remarked upon the most excellent brickwork, windows and doors and then paused to ask if we still had those deadly geese. I sighed and then showed him my numerous scars from those fierce creatures.

9:22am: He admitted that he had to get to work (I really needed the bathroom . . . how many brews had I had now?). He looked at the ladder and said, "It's in the wrong place (he then proceeded to move the ladder) . . . that's better, you will be able to reach more of the wall now without having to get down from the ladder to re-locate it." I thanked him (after all, what did I know? He was a proper painter and decorator!). He drove off and I visited the bathroom.

9:37am: One bathroom stop and another brew later, I climbed the ladder to start painting again and then it happened . . . but it seemed to be in slow motion, it took such a long time!

"Long time!" and the things we do!

1 Kings 18:1–2 says,

> *"After a **long time** ... the word of the LORD came to Elijah: 'Go and present yourself to Ahab, and I will send rain on the land.' So Elijah went to present himself to Ahab. Now the famine was severe in Samaria ..."*
>
> (emphasis added)

Verses 45–46 say,

> *"Meanwhile, the sky grew black with clouds, the wind rose, a heavy rain came on ..."*

I have discovered that the concept of a "LONG TIME" is a relative thing. In fact, the exact same duration of time can either be a "SHORT TIME" or a "LONG TIME" depending on what you are doing. For example,

- Two weeks holiday in Cyprus felt like such a "SHORT TIME", but two weeks camping in England in the rain felt like such a "LONG TIME"!
- Three hours on a game console seems like such a "SHORT TIME", but three hours in an exam feels like such a ... (all together now) ... "LONG TIME"!
- Half an hour's sleep is such a "SHORT TIME", but half an hour in the dentist's chair feels like such a "LONG TIME".

I meet many people every year who feel like it's been such a LONG TIME since something good happened to them. Or it feels like such a LONG TIME since God spoke to them or blessed them. Or it's such a LONG TIME since they could relax, or laugh, or had money to spend on things.

The story in 1 Kings chapter 18 starts with a LONG TIME since something happened (in this case – rain), but finishes with *"heavy rain"* in verse 46.

God wants to move you from LONG TIME to SHORT TIME. He wants you to move from "drought" to "rain", from "hoping" to "receiving", from "wishing that it will happen for you one day" (whatever that "happen" may be) to actually "living out your dreams".

Too many people in the LONG TIME season make the wrong decisions, try to short cut the purposes of God for their lives and end up saying, "If I knew what was gonna happen next, I never would have made those decisions ... I should have just carried on doing the right thing for long enough."

What do you do if it feels like such a LONG TIME since something happened in your life that lined up with your dreams of who you want to be and what you want to accomplish? There are four things.

1. Read 1 Kings chapter 18

Go on – do it! Forty-six verses ... have you done it? These next three points won't make sense if you don't ...

2. Make a decision

In verse 21 of this duel Elijah challenges the people to make a decision. We read that, *"Elijah went before the people and said, 'How long will you waver between two opinions?' "* The Hebrew word[1] for "waver" literally means "to be crippled".

The people thought they were smart. They worshipped God sometimes and then at other times they worshipped Baal. They were "hedging their bets" – not wanting to upset either God or Baal, so they worshipped them both.

Elijah was saying, "The nation is spiritually, socially and financially crippled because you are indecisive!" The New Living Translation says, *"How much longer will you waver, hobbling between two opinions?"* (emphasis added).

James 1:8 tells us that a *"double-minded"* (indecisive) person is *"unstable in all his ways!"* (NKJV). Indecision creates instability (difficulty) in all areas of life. Sometimes your "problem" may not be *the* problem. Perhaps you have spent time trying to fix a certain area of your life that doesn't actually need fixing. If you are indecisive in any aspect of your life, it will create instability and difficulty in ALL areas of your life! The key is to become a decision maker!

Indecision makes you tired. When I pluck up the courage to go clothes shopping, I stand in front of the clothes racks willing something to jump out at me. If I have to wade my way through rails of clothes that are jammed in tight, I soon get tired because there is too much choice and my energy is sapped! Tiredness is a bi-product of indecision.

Indecision restrains the blessing of God on your life. Jesus said,

> *"I know your deeds, that you are **neither cold nor hot**. I wish you were **either one or the other**! So, because you are lukewarm – **neither hot nor cold** – I am about to spit you out of my mouth."*
>
> (Revelation 3:15–16, emphasis added)

The challenge is, "Make a decision!"

Decide about God. If God is God, then choose Him. But don't waver, don't limp into church, school, college or work! Walk tall and strong having made a decision that God is God. Decide about Church. If you go to church, make it so. Don't go one week and then miss three. Make your church, your church! Decide about your career. Decide about your future plans. Decide about that relationship. Decide about your education. Decide about your finances …. what are you waiting for?

Three keys to making good choices

▶ *1. Get Talking*

> *"Where there is no counsel, the people fall;*
> *but in the multitude of counsellors there is safety."*
> (Proverbs 11:14 NKJV)

One of the best ways to make a good decision is to talk it through with people. The Bible says that there is wisdom in a multitude of counsellors. Just make sure they are the right multitude! There may be a multitude of people at the local sumo wrestling convention, but they may not be the best people to speak to regarding your weight loss programme. Find trustworthy, honest people who you admire and seek their input in your decision-making process!

▶ *2. Get Knowledge*

Recently my wife and I bought some property in another nation. We had no idea how to go about it or what it would cost and so we got knowledge.

The Bible says,

> *"Of what use is money in the hand of a fool,*
> *since he has no desire to get wisdom?"*
>
> (Proverbs 17:16)

We went to property presentations by various companies and we talked to as many people as we could who had invested in property overseas. We also read a lot of information. Proverbs 9:12 says, *"If you are wise, your wisdom will reward you ... "*

▶ *3. The Feel Good factor*
The Bible says,

> *"Do not be anxious about anything, but in everything,*
> *by prayer and petition, with thanksgiving, present your*
> *requests to God. And the peace of God, which transcends*
> *all understanding, will guard your hearts and your minds*
> *in Christ Jesus."*   (Philippians 4:6–8)

The peace of God is amazing. You can have it even if all hell is breaking loose in your life. When someone close to me died, I remember being very sad and yet inside there was a peace. It makes no sense, you shouldn't really have it and yet it is there.

Decision making is best when, after talking it through and gaining knowledge, you have a peace on the inside that confirms your decision!

3. Watch your words

The third thing you need to do when you are in a LONG

TIME situation is watch your words! Hebrews 11:3 says, *"By faith we understand that the world was framed by the word of God..."*[2] In the same way that God's words framed the world, so too will your words create your world! They shape your path and plot your destiny. Your tongue is like having "dynamite in the dentures"! Proverbs 18:21 says, *"Death and life are in the power of the tongue..."* (NKJV).

In the story, Elijah is confronted on three fronts and he speaks appropriately to each.

▶ *(a) He is confronted by the opinion of others!*
In verse 17 the king calls Elijah the *"troubler of Israel!"* This was not true. In actual fact it was the king who was creating havoc in the nation. Elijah replies, "I am not that person!"

In life you will be blamed and accused of all sorts of things. People will attempt to label you as one thing or another. They may label you as popular, a freak, ridiculous or unique. But it is important to know who you are and what you represent.[3]

▶ *(b) He is confronted with fear*
In verse 24 Elijah says, *"The god who answers by fire – he is God!"* What would have happened if God didn't act on his behalf? I am sure that Elijah considered that fact. And yet, when confronted with the fear of what might go wrong, he chose to act in faith (more later) and expected God to turn up and do something.

Next time you are confronted with fear, or any other negative emotions, choose to expect God to step in the ring and act on your behalf, just like He did with Elijah.

Fear is simply a thought, feeling or action based on what *might* happen! Faith is also a thought, feeling or action based on what *might* happen. While you are in NOW, waiting for your NEXT, choose faith over fear and watch God act for you!

▶ *(c) He is confronted with an opportunity*

In verse 37 Elijah expresses his confidence that God will act on his behalf. This is a massive opportunity for God to show up, show off and show how – and He does exactly that!

When you are presented with opportunities, choose to speak the right things over them. In other words, expect the best! Expect God! Expect the "Wow" of a supernatural God doing a supernatural thing. Too many people, when presented with an opportunity, speak the worst and expect the least. The Bible says in Ephesians 3:20 that God is *"Him who is able to do immeasurably more than all we ask or imagine!"*

Whatever opportunity you are facing, remember that your words frame your world. They shape your destiny and plot your path! Speak words of faith and "God-expectancy" over each opportunity and watch and be amazed at what God will do.

4. Have faith in God

Elijah gives the maximum amount of time to the false prophets as they call out to their god to answer by fire. The Bible says,

> *"About noontime Elijah began mocking them. 'You'll have to shout louder,' he scoffed, 'for surely he is a god! Perhaps he is daydreaming, or is relieving himself. Or maybe he is away on a trip, or is asleep and needs to be wakened!'"* (verse 27 NLT)

I love that! Imagine the false prophet's god relieving himself (taking a leak). That cracks me up!

The prophets shouted all the more. They even cut themselves, but nothing happened. Finally, Elijah stepped up (read verses 30–38) and this is what he did...

- *Verse 30*: He called the people together to watch what God was going to do! The people needed to see this one!
- *Verses 30–31*: He built an altar using twelve stones. The number twelve is the sign of unity in the Bible. Psalm 133:1 says that when we are in unity, God "commands" a blessing on the people. By taking twelve stones Elijah was making the statement, "I know these people are crippled and half-hearted, but after this God-act, they will all turn to the one true God!"
- *Verse 33*: He put the bull on the altar. Excuse the pun, but the best place to put "bull" is on the altar of worship and let God deal with it. Too many people talk about their problems for years and years. "Bull" belongs on the altar.
- *Verses 33–34*: He makes it interesting. Elijah pours four jars of water on the sacrifice three times (that's TWELVE again). My experience tells me that if you want a fire you don't put water near it! Water puts out fire, surely Elijah knew that. Why make it harder for God? Incidentally, there was a famine and a drought in the land. The very thing they needed was water! He actually poured out the very thing they needed. You can imagine people thinking, "What is he doing? There isn't enough to drink anyway without him wasting water!" And yet, Elijah was sowing on the altar of worship the very thing he was believing for! If you lack money, sow it in your tithes

and offerings. If you lack friendship/time/energy/love, then sow it because the Bible says *"A man reaps what he sows"* (Galatians 6:7).

- *Verses 36–37*: He steps forward and says, "Come on God, now it's Your turn to step up and show the people that You are God!"

Elijah had the faith to believe that God would do something great and God did something great!

Finishing off the third Next now – so I can get onto what happened next

In verses 39, 41 and 46, we read that people stopped limping and they started running towards the life God had destined for them.

When I was twenty I was living in Australia, saving money for my Bible College tuition. I had only just returned to Australia after living for five years in Manchester, England, and so I took the first available job. That job was in an aluminium foundry in the outback of Australia. I would wake up at 5:30am to travel to work and begin the job at 7:00am. One of my jobs was to wear the leather spats (protective clothing), as we stirred and added new aluminium into the furnaces. The combination of the molten metal and the heat of the Australian sun merging in the corrugated iron sheds meant that the temperature would reach in excess of 50 degrees Celsius. By 7:30am I would be dripping with sweat and we would keep that up until we finished work at 5:30pm each day. The only relief in the day came at 3:30pm. We would strip our clothes off until we were only wearing shorts and stand in the wheat fields. We would watch a wall of water race towards us with lightning speed. It was the daily ten-minute torrential downpour. That rain would cool us down. It was awesome!

In Elijah's story the LONG TIME drought breaks and Elijah hears the sound of heavy rain approaching (verse 45).

Perhaps just like Elijah, it has felt like such a long time since God spoke to you or blessed you. Or maybe it's been such a long time since you could relax, or laugh, or had money to spend on things.

1 Kings chapter 18 starts with a LONG TIME since something happened, but finishes with heavy rain.

God wants to move you from "LONG TIME" to "SHORT TIME". He wants you to move from "wishing that it will happen for you one day" (whatever that "happen" may be) to actually "living out your dreams".

Perhaps just like the people in 1 Kings 18, you are limping in different areas of your life, why not,

▶ *(a) Make a decision by*
- Talking it through
- Gaining knowledge
- Confirming it using the "feel good" factor

▶ *(b) Watch your words*
- Remember your words frame your world

▶ *(c) Have faith in God*
- Create space for God to do what only He can do

Coming up:

"Homer Simpson ruined the party!"

Notes

1. Most of the Old Testament was written in Hebrew. The New Testament was written in Greek.
2. The Douay-Rheims Bible.
3. Read the second book in this series. It is called *If I Had a Face Like Yours* (New Wine Press, 2006). The chapter entitled "Decide to be a spaceship" deals with this in detail!

Making it real for you!

1. Are you decisive or indecisive?

   ....

2. What are the three areas you find it most difficult to make decisions about?

   (a) ....

   ....

   (b) ....

   ....

   (c) ....

   ....

3. How will changing the way you speak help you?

   ....

   ....

   ....

   ....

   ....

4. In what area of your life can you create space for God to step in and do a miracle?

   ....

   ....

   ....

   ....

   ....

Someone once said,

"Dolphins: Don't trust a species that's always smiling. They're up to something!"

Next #4

If I knew what happened next, I would...

...have double checked!

9:37am: One bathroom stop and another brew later, I climbed the ladder to start painting again and then it happened ... but it seemed to be in slow motion, it took such a long time!

Unbelievable! I thought my mate was a proper painter and decorator! It was his fault! He moved the ladder to a "better" position, but when I climbed the ladder it hadn't been "footed" properly! The ladder moved and that new five-litre tub of paint slipped off the stick and fell towards the ground. I tried to grab it, but I missed! It was like slow motion. My brain responded too slowly, the paint pot hit the sidewalk and exploded. The paint shot out of the tub, splashed across the new front door and completely covered the new window frame and glass! I looked at Pat. The geese were the least of our troubles now.

I slowly descended the ladder, assessing the carnage with each step. Then the magnitude of the situation hit me. As I reached the bottom rung I looked into the hairdressing salon ... NO! Why didn't they have the door closed? Didn't they realize there were workman on site? The paint had not only covered the outside of the hairdressing salon, but it had also shot inside it. Five customers were slowly getting to their feet. The one closest to the door was wearing a tweed suit! He was covered in paint. The paint covered each of the lenses of his glasses and there was paint dripping from his nose! Each of the customers in turn had paint on their clothing! Needless to say, the language coming out of their mouths made me blush. Why didn't I check the position of the ladder before I climbed it?!

Homer Simpson and the party!

Take a moment to read 2 Kings 2:1–18.

Verse 1 begins, *"When the LORD was about to ... "* We have to understand that God is always "about to do" something. All He needs are the people who will say, "God, here I am, use me!"

In 1993 I lived in Sydney. My best mate and I decided to go into the city centre to hear the announcement of who had won the right to host the 2000 Olympics. The Sydney council had set up BBQ areas, stages for bands to play on, drinks wagons and large screens around the city centre so people could see the announcement. If Sydney won the right to host the games the city would have a party to end all parties. If Sydney did not win the rights to host the games ... the city would party anyway! We decided we wanted to be in the middle of the party! As the day of the announcement drew near, however, we were tired and after consulting the TV listings we decided to stay at home, watch *The Simpsons*, and then flip the channel to see the announcement live on TV. We grabbed our chips and coke, watched and laughed at *The Simpsons* (I love Itchy and Scratchy!) and then changed the channel just in time to hear the announcement. I'll never forget the moment when the President of the International Olympic Committee said, " ... and the winner is ... Sydney!"

At that moment the whole city centre began to party. Fireworks, bands and free barbecues. It was an amazing party! My friend looked at me and said, "Mate, we missed it!" We had the chance to be a part of something incredible, but chose instead to be comfortable.

God wants to do something awesome with your life and you need to make a decision not to miss it. Jesus said in John 10:10 that He came to give life and life to the full. Too many people settle for "life", when in actual fact God wants you to have "life to the full!" In others words, your life becomes the party that my friend and I missed out on.

At the hairdressers the paint fell because the ladder was positioned poorly! My painter friend had placed the ladder on uneven ground and I didn't check its position. The result was disastrous!

In life we also need to position ourselves correctly so that we are the right people in the right place at the right time. Faith is not just an emotion, a feeling, or some abstract concept – it is also a "position", so that we don't have to say, "We missed the party!"

There are six questions from 2 Kings 2:1–18 we need to ask ourselves if we want to position ourselves correctly NOW, so that our NEXT has a better chance of being a success!

1. Who are you with?

Verse 1 says, "... *Elijah and Elisha* ..."

When I was a student we used to have study triplets! Three of us would get together to study for our exams, but we would each study different parts of the subject. We would then teach each other the material we had learnt so that together we had studied the whole subject. If one of my study partners hadn't done his job well, it would affect the way I wrote the answers in the exam. Our success or failure was determined by each other!

It is exactly the same in life. You need to choose friends who will help and encourage you as you pursue God and your career! If you want to be a world changer, hang out with those who are! Who are you with and how can they help you be all you can be?

In 2 Kings 2 Elisha was positioning himself to receive something from God. God was about to do something and Elisha was going to be right there when He did.

When you are alone

In Judges 18:1-2, 7 and 27-28 it says,

> *"In those days Israel had no king ... the tribe of the Danites was seeking a place of their own ... So the Danites sent five warriors ... to spy out the land and explore it ... They told them, 'Go, explore the land' ... the five men left and came to Laish, where they saw that the people were living in safety ... **and had no relationship with anyone else** ...* [they] *went on to Laish ... attacked them with the sword ... there was no one to rescue them because they ... **had no relationship with anyone else.**"*   (emphasis added)

The Danites[1] had attacked other places and lost, but they won in Laish because they (the people of Laish) *"had no relationship with anyone else."* It was the lack of someone being with them that led to Laish being defeated. They were not with anyone and because of that they were isolated, weak and vulnerable!

Scooter or rocket?

I once heard a preacher put it this way, "When I was little, my mum and dad bought me a scooter. I loved that scooter! It was red! It was fast and I could drive up and down our driveway. Then my mum and dad bought me a bike. I could ride up and down the road on that bike. Then I got a bigger bike and I could ride the five blocks to school. Then I got a car and I could drive across the country. Then I got on a plane and I could fly to the other side of the world. I've never been on a rocket, but imagine how far I could get in that!"

The point is simple: the vehicle you attach yourself to will determine how far you get in life!

The question is, "Who are you with?"

2. Where are you going?

Verse 1 says Elijah and Elisha were "... *on their way* ... " It was easy for God to use Elisha because he was already on his way pursuing his destiny and purpose!

My friend Alan had a very cool car when I was eighteen years old. One day, as he was pulling into a petrol station, he saw some of the girls from the college hanging around outside the shop. Being very cool, as he turned into the service station he turned off his engine so he could glide into the forecourt to get some petrol. He didn't realize that when he turned off the engine the power steering would cut out! Instead of coasting in alongside the petrol pump, he ran right into the pump, knocked it over, and looked very silly as the girls pointed and laughed at him!

Alan couldn't steer the car because the engine wasn't on! It's the same with God and us. It is very difficult for God to direct us if we are doing nothing! Our spirit is like the engine of a car. We need to make sure it's running by praying, reading the Bible, serving in church and living for God to the best of our ability. When we do that, God sees and is easily able to direct us and position us so that we don't miss what He is going to do!

When Jesus called the disciples to follow Him in Matthew 4:19, He chose people who were busy, not hermits living a monastic lifestyle! He took men who were passionate about fishing for fish and he re-directed their passion to fishing for men.

Keep doing what you are doing. Study at university and college. Take that part-time job, but be ready for God to re-direct you. My youth pastors have degrees, but neither of them are using their qualifications to do what they are doing now. God re-directed them. But understand that nothing is wasted.

What are you doing? If you are doing nothing, "Look busy, Jesus is coming!" (I love that bumper sticker!)

3. What obstacles do you face?

In verses 2, 4 and 6 Elijah says to Elisha *"... stay here ..."*

Elisha was busy pursuing what he felt was God's plan for his life, BUT he was continually being told to stop. This was a huge obstacle for him. The man he respected the most was telling him to stop. What obstacles do you face? If your life is going to be significant for God, you will face obstacles!

When Sophia and I moved to England in 1996 to pursue God's plans for our lives, my Dad died suddenly! It was a huge shock! My Mum was now a widow living in Australia. Should I stay in Australia or move to England as planned? It was very difficult to make the decision. The obstacle seemed huge. We talked things through with mum and delayed our move to England by six weeks. It was a very emotional time and it would have been easy to stay in Australia forever!

I put off my "future" by six weeks, but some of you reading this have put things off totally because of the obstacles you are facing. Maybe it's time to get moving again!

Obstacles come in all shapes and sizes. Maybe your parents fight or are divorced. Perhaps you are misunderstood, or maybe you don't understand. But don't ever say the obstacle is too big. It never is! (I'll show you why.)

4. What's your passion?

In verses 2, 4, and 6 Elisha showed his passion by saying, *"I will not leave you . . . "*

Proverbs 23:7 says, *"As* [a man] *thinks – so is he."* In other words, your life will be led by your most dominant thoughts! You will become the very thing you pursue so passionately in your heart!

Proverbs 4:23 says, *"Keep your heart with all diligence, for out of it spring the issues of life"* (NKJV). The word "issues" here literally means "borders or boundaries"!

If you are really passionate about something and continually talk to God about it, and always do your utmost to live for God, then the boundaries of your life will be massive. When you face obstacles you don't stop at them and say, "Oh no, it's too big." Instead you say, "The borders of my heart are massive, this obstacle can't contain me. I'll just walk around it."

5. What's your request?

In verse 9 Elijah, knowing he is about to die, says to Elisha, *"Tell me, what can I do for you before I am taken from you?"* Elisha replies, *"Let me inherit a double portion of your spirit."* Elisha's request was audacious – God loves that!

It's okay to ask big things from God! Ephesians 3:20 says, *"Now to him* [God] *who is able to do immeasurably more than all we ask or imagine . . . "* What do you imagine your life could become? What do you imagine God could do in your life? He says, "I can do more!"

In the New Testament there was a woman who had been bleeding for many years. When she heard Jesus was in town, she pushed through the crowd and touched Jesus. Jesus said, *"Who touched me?"* The disciples said, "There's loads of people pushing forward to touch you!" But Jesus said, "No, there was one person in the crowd who REALLY touched Me!" What happened? Loads of people were asking Jesus things; loads of people were there; but only one woman made a request of significance. She got healed that day.

Make your requests – significant requests – of God! God says, "What can I do for you?" You need to say, "God, I don't want to miss out, I want to be there when the party starts … when You bring revival to my city/school/friends. In fact God, here I am, use me!"

6. What are you gonna do?

The last question is found in verse 14. Elisha has now come back to the place where the water had parted previously, but the problem now is that Elijah is no longer around to do a miracle. People are watching Elisha and he comes out with the classic line, *"Where now is the LORD, the God of Elijah?"*

In the same way people were watching Elisha, your friends, school mates and family are watching you. When was the last time you were in a place where you needed God to come through for you?

Following God is an adventure because sometimes you feel the prompting of God to do something ridiculous, even bizarre. But when you act after hearing God tell you to do something, amazing things happen. The Bible calls them miracles! The God of Elijah and Elisha is your God! If He could do amazing things through them, He can do them through you too!

Finishing off the fourth Next now – so I can get onto what happened next

I hated missing that party in Sydney. Likewise, I would hate to reach the end of my life and say "I missed it! I had the opportunity to live a significant life, but I settled for comfort instead!"

Let's not be a generation that misses what God wants to do. Let's position ourselves right! How? Remember,

- Who are you with?
- Where are you going?
- What obstacles do you face?
- What's your passion?
- What's your request?
- What are you gonna do?

It's not a magic formula, but maybe it'll help you be the right person, in the right place at the right time. I'm looking forward to seeing you in the middle of the party! You bring the sausages and I'll bring the drinks!

Coming up:

"Are they naked?"

Note

1. The Danites were not Danish (Denmark) as one of my students once thought! The Danites were the tribe of Dan. See Genesis chapter 49.

Making it real for you!

1. Who are you connected with?

   ....
   ....

2. Where are you going?

   ....
   ....

3. What obstacles do you face?

   ....
   ....
   ....

4. What's your passion?

   ....
   ....

5. What's your request?

   ....
   ....

6. What are you gonna do?

   ....
   ....
   ....
   ....
   ....

Someone once said,

"After hearing two eyewitness accounts of the same accident, you begin to wonder about history."

Next #5

If I knew what happened next, I would...

...not have rushed off with such haste!

9:38am: The hairdresser, who was at one point completely speechless by what he had seen, suddenly exploded with the venom of a British Bulldog who had been stung on the tongue by a wasp!

He was swearing and gesticulating in a general manner until he caught sight of me doing absolutely nothing. (I was in shock!) He shouted, "Go and get some White Spirit to clean this mess up!" I couldn't think straight! "Yes sir," I said. I ran to the van, searching high and low. I would gladly trade this moment for a fight with the geese. Would you believe it? There was no White Spirit. I ran to Pat, "What do I do?" "Drive to the yard and get some quick!" he said.

9:40am: I jumped into the van and drove at lightning speed. In the rush, I forgot to pick up my bag.

9:42am: I arrived at the yard to discover I'd left my bag back at the salon. Yep, you guessed it, the keys to the yard were in the bag.

9:45am: Arrived back at the hairdressers. The carnage was worse than I thought. Pat and the hairdresser ran out to meet me. Sheepishly I admitted to having forgotten my keys. Amidst many shouts and the host of curious onlookers who had gathered to witness the spectacle, I picked up my bag and set off back to the yard. But things were about to get worse!

What's the rush?

You can't blame me can you? I forgot the keys! Yeah, but there was so much going on. The pressure was immense. Let me list the issues I was facing.

1. I had people shouting at me
2. The geese had attacked me again
3. I was embarrassed
4. I had ruined people's clothes and glasses
5. I had embarrassed the people in the salon
6. It would probably be a while before my next brew
7. My boss was gonna kill me (perhaps sack me!)
8. I forgot my keys
9. I couldn't find the White Spirit
10. I had to go back to the yard, alone, where the geese would probably attack me

Are they naked?

Sophia and I wanted a holiday! Rhodes seemed like the place to go to, so we went to the travel agent and spent three and a half hours with them searching the computer to find the holiday at the right price.

The travel agent suggested other places that were within our budget, but we had our hearts set on Rhodes. Finally, we found a resort, much to the relief of the agent and booked a holiday.

Two weeks later we set off on a two-week vacation in "Rhodes". After three days, however, something happened to make me realize we weren't in Rhodes after all!

Each morning I went for a run along the beach. On my first two days on the island I had run to a particular point on the peninsula, and so on the third day I set off to do exactly the same. As I neared the peninsula, I saw something that shocked me a little ... well, a lot! I saw an elderly couple running towards me and I thought to myself, "Wait a minute! Are they naked?" Sure enough, they were! I had to make a choice. What do I do? Do I run past and smile politely, OR do I turn back? I still had about half a mile to run to get to the peninsula. "Yep, I can do it!" I thought. But a few more paces and I quickly changed my mind. I stopped my run short and turned back towards our apartment.

When I reached the main road that led to our apartment, I stopped running and started walking to catch my breath. It was about 7:30am. Most of the locals and tourists on this particular Greek island were still asleep, but there was one youth walking in front of me. That person turned around, looked at me and said, "Glyn?" (more later!)

What it took to get me on the planet

My genealogy began before the world began (Jeremiah 1:5). Let me tell you the modern genealogy of my family.

My Granddad was born in the valleys of South Wales in the late 1800s. He worked in the Tin Works until 1914 when World War 1 started. Granddad lied about his age and joined the British Army at sixteen. He fought in some of the fiercest battles in the front line trenches of the war. He worked as a blacksmith, but also had to "go over the top" of the trenches to fight in battles like The Somme and Ypres. On many occasions as he fought, the man on either side of him fell in battle. The second time he got wounded he was sent back to Great Britain to recover and on returning to the battlefront, discovered that eighty percent of his friends had been killed in battle. He, however, managed to survive the war years. After the war Granddad felt forced to join the communist party as the communists were the only ones he could find who were prepared to help the returning war heroes financially.

In 1935 my father was born, a twin, in a quiet little street in a quiet little village in South Wales. Men would call at the house to discuss communist issues and both my dad and uncle had the opportunity to listen in to these meetings. One day my dad was playing football with some of the lads from a local church. During the game Dad was responsible for breaking the leg of one of the guys playing the game. As a result, they invited Dad to go to church and on the next Sunday, my dad said "yes" to Jesus. My mum made the same decision around six years later.

Later Dad trained as an armature winder[1] and after he qualified he travelled to London to attend Bible College for two years. After graduating, Dad moved back to Wales, married Mum, and pastored a church in a small town. He stayed there for two years. Whilst there, he had two motor-bike accidents, leaving him in hospital and recovering for approximately twelve months of his two-year stay.

Mum and Dad then moved to Gateshead in the north of

England where my sister, Sian, was born. Several years later they moved to Manchester where I was born!

At the age of two my family moved to Australia where I grew up in a nice little, conservative city of around 80,000 people. I blew up a dog,[2] played cricket on a church roof,[3] wore my sister's bra on my head during her first date,[4] swam naked[5] and then ... aged fifteen, moved back to Manchester, UK. After few years in Manchester, I moved back to Australia to attend Bible College, met Sophia[6] in a small country city, lived just outside Sydney, got married and then moved back to Sheffield, England. More recently, after eleven years serving in a great church in Sheffield, we have moved to Manchester to build a great city centre church. (This is the very abbreviated version of events that did not include prophetic words, little conversations that sowed big seeds, encounters with God etc.) I am living smack bang in the middle of God's plans and purposes for my life. In fact, I have learnt the very important lesson that ...

I SERVE THE MAN WITH THE PLAN

Too often we fall into the trap of rushing around in life, making quick decisions and panicking because things are not working according to "our plans". Proverbs 16:9 says,

> *"In his heart a man plans his course,*
> *but the LORD determines his steps."*

I have met people all over the world who have made major mistakes because of a fear that things weren't going to work out. Instead of being confident in God's ability to "finish the good work He started" (see Philippians 1:6), they acted

85

impulsively, taking their destiny into their own hands without giving God the opportunity to do something.

If you live with the understanding that you "serve the Man with the plan", you will learn to relax and be confident in God's ability to work in you and through you and on your behalf.

When did Jesus get so weak and insipid?

1 Timothy 2:5 says,

> *"For there is one God and one mediator between God and men, **the man** Christ Jesus . . . "*   (emphasis added)

Jesus is not any man, He is THE MAN! Perhaps you have heard that the Bible calls Jesus the "King OF kings" and the "Lord OF lords"? I've got another one for you . . . He is the "Man OF men!"

One of the greatest strategies of the devil in attacking Jesus has got to be the way in which he has inspired painters over the centuries to portray Jesus as some weak, insipid person! The majority of modern men would stand in front of a picture of Jesus in the great religious museums of the world and admit to "never wanting to look like Him!"

Naturally speaking, Jesus was a carpenter by trade. Naturally speaking He would have been adept at carrying heavy loads and working long hours of manual labour, creating great feats of carpentry.

Spiritually speaking Jesus was, "all God and all man"[7] at the same time. Not only was He a strong man by virtue of His trade, He was also all of God in man at the same time. That's why the Bible calls Him, "THE MAN".

The Man in the Old Testament

In the story of David's mighty men (2 Samuel 23:8–12), it says that Josheb was a Takhemonite, Eleazar was an Ahohite and Shammah was a Harrarite. In other words, one was from Canada, one from Peru and the other from India! (Not literally, it's just that they were gathered from different tribes and nations.) The Bible says that as David's mighty men they were "with each other". Somehow they were drawn together from different parts of the world to be with each other, to fight side by side, to spend a season in life together.

They were brought from different places to be with each other. Why? Because they served the man with the plan!

Make no mistake, Jesus is all through the Old Testament. You may have thought that Jesus only appeared on the scene when He was born in Bethlehem. The Bible however, speaks of the concept of the "Trinity".[8] Colossians chapter 1 says " ... *all things were created by him and for him ... "* The HIM that these verses are speaking about is Jesus! Jesus was involved in the creation of the world!

In Genesis 22:14 we read about "Jehovah Jireh" meaning "the Lord our Provider". In Psalm 23 read about "Jehovah Rophe" – "The Lord our Shepherd". In fact, every time we read about "Jehovah" in the Old Testament, we are confronted with "THE MAN".

When the Old Testament was translated into Greek (known as the Septuagint), the Hebrew word "Jehovah" was translated as *Kyrios* meaning "Lord". The only person in the Trinity with the name "Lord" is Jesus! Jesus is all through the Old Testament and the men and women in the Old Testament "served the man with the plan".

The Man in the New Testament

Acts 16:6–10 says that Paul was kept by the Holy Spirit from preaching in a certain place and that the *"Spirit of Jesus"* would not allow him and his companions to go into another place. So they concluded that God had called them to preach the gospel in still another place.

Why did it happen like this? Because they were serving the man with the plan.

The Man in my life

Looking at my life now, I can see that it could have gone wrong at any given point. If those bullets had been an inch to the left in World War 1, then my granddad would have been killed and I wouldn't be here today. Why did he end up recovering in Britain when he did? If Dad hadn't broken the leg of a guy from church playing football that day, then I wouldn't be here today and you wouldn't be sitting on the toilet reading this page! Dad could easily have died in those motor-bike accidents. What would have happened if I went to Bible College in England? I would never have met Sophia whose family originated in Chile (South America). Why did they move to Australia? Why did I meet her on that particular day, in that particular place? Too many things had to go right in my life and the generations before me to make that meeting possible. Too many things could easily have gone wrong, but they didn't ... why? Because I had to write a book called *If I Knew What Happened Next*! The major lesson I have learnt in my life is *"I serve the Man with a plan!"*

"The Man" on the Greek Island

Remember the story? That person turned around, looked at me and said, "Glyn?"

Several years prior to this, I had been involved in pioneering a youth group in a church in a major city. We started with eleven young people and this young person who now faced me on the street (we'll call him Matt), on this Greek island that was not Rhodes, was one of those eleven youth. Eight years into building this youth ministry, Matt ran off, never to be seen by any of us again. BUT ... I ended up on an island I wasn't meant to be on, in a destination I was never meant to be at, in order to meet him again. I should have been on Rhodes. Why was I now running up a beach, being confronted by old naked people, being forced to turn and run back to my apartment, causing me to be standing on this particular main road at this particular moment in order to bump into this guy who had run away from God? Because *"I serve the Man with a plan!"* You can try to run from God, but God will always turn up! Incidentally, the reason that Matt was up so early that morning, walking up that particular road, was because, he also *"serves the Man with the plan!"*

Finishing off the fifth Next now – so I can get onto what happened next

It's time to relax a little bit! Matthew 6:25 says, *"Do not worry..."* Why? Because you serve the Man with the plan! I don't know what your plan is, but I do know it's a good one. Jeremiah 29:11 says,

> *"For I know the plans I have for you ... plans to prosper you and not to harm you, plans to give you hope and a future."*

The next time you are tempted to do something rash, rushed or impulsive, remember, *"you serve the Man with a plan"*.

It's okay to make your own plans, but don't lose your sanity or faith if your plans don't go according to plan. Remember, Proverbs 16:9 says,

> *"In his heart a man plans his course,*
> *but the LORD determines his steps."*

You may not quite understand what is going on in your life right now, but just remember, "the Man has a plan", and that plan is a GOOD plan.

The Man is not cruel though. He doesn't want to keep it all to Himself. He wants to show you part of the plan too. How does He do it? Simple...

> *"Your word is a lamp to my feet*
> *and a light for my path."* (Psalm 119:105)

God's word is a lamp ... and light...

Don't forget, when you read the Bible, make sure you B.U.R.P! (Sorry, you will have to read *If I Had a Face Like Yours*, the second book in this series to understand that one!)

Everything is cool, you serve *"the Man with a plan!"*

Coming up:

"The man hit my plane with a sledgehammer!"

Notes _____

1. Armature-winders locate broken parts of an electric motor of which the coils are burnt out or damaged. They will either repair or replace them with a new ones, or completely rewind all the coils.

2. Glyn Barrett, *If I Was the Devil*, Sovereign World Publishing, 2004.

3. Ibid.

4. Ibid.

5. Ibid.

6. Sophia's family are from Chile in South America.

7. The theological term for this is "hypostatic union" = all God and all man at the same time!

8. The term "Trinity" was first used by a man called Tertullian in the second century AD to best describe the concept of the Godhead as three in one!

Making it real for you!

1. Why do you make mistakes when you rush?

    ....

    ....

    ....

2. What do you know about your family history that shows
    "the Man has a plan?"

    ....

    ....

    ....

    ....

3. What three ways does knowing "the Man has a plan"
    help you?

    (a) ....

    ....

    (b) ....

    ....

    (c) ....

    ....

4. Next time you are tempted to do something rash, rushed
    or impulsive, what are you going to remember to do?

    ....

    ....

    ....

Someone once said,

"Don't worry about the world
coming to an end today.
It is already tomorrow
in Australia!"

Next #6

If I knew what happened next, I would...

...have checked the roof!

9:45am: Arrived back at the hairdressers. The carnage was worse than I thought. Pat and the hairdresser ran out to meet me. Sheepishly I admitted to having forgotten my keys. Amidst many shouts and the host of curious onlookers who had gathered to witness the spectacle, I picked up my bag and set off back to the yard. But things were about to get worse!

9:47am: Driving in a panic now! I can't believe the way my day is turning out ... desperately need a brew ... not gonna get one for ages yet.

9:48am: Not far from the yard. What's that noise? I looked in the rear view mirror to witness an aluminium pair of ladders cartwheel down the main road behind me. I quickly had a mental flash back to earlier in the morning when I removed the first pair of ladders so I could paint the wall above the door of the hairdressers. Why didn't I check the roof before I drove at breakneck speed down the highway? Come to think of it, why didn't the ladders fall off on my first trip to the yard when I forgot my keys?

9:48.30am: Skidded to a stop. Ran down the highway, picked up the ladder and threw it into the back of the van! Jumped back in the van and raced to the yard.

9:49am: Opened the gates at the yard ... kicked the geese (secretly plotted their demise) ... located white spirits ... kicked the geese again...

9:50am: Locked gate ... drove back to the salon.

9:52am: Used the white spirits to clean the paint ... WHY ISN'T THE WHITE SPIRIT WORKING? Yep, the paint was water-based and could be hosed off. Why didn't I read the label on the paint tin?!

That day consisted of a whole series of incidents that led from one to another until finally the situation got closer to being resolved. If I hadn't raced off to the yard to get the White Spirit, I never would have discovered that the paint was water-based and therefore easier to wash off than first expected. Sure, there were other little things that took place along the way, like ladders falling off the van and me kicking the geese, but I had to get through one moment which then led me to another which finally led me to the end of the day!

The Sledgehammer

I was twenty-four years of age and I had just boarded a plane in Bangkok, Thailand. The plane taxied to its take off position and as the engines revved and the plane began to gain speed on the runway, the engine next to where I was sitting made a loud noise. I had flown enough to realize that planes were not meant to make that kind of sound ... old cars maybe, tractors perhaps, even paint pots falling from a great height or geese being strangled, but not Boeing 747s!

The pilot braked and then steered the plane into an aircraft hanger. We sat for three hours whilst technicians, at least I think they were technicians, performed some kind of technical (after all, they were technicians) function on the plane. We sat in the blistering heat inside the plane inside the aircraft hanger; the conditions were pretty bad.

At one point I glanced out of the window and saw a small Thai gentleman wearing flip-flops and a singlet top, hitting the engine with what looked like a sledgehammer. I must admit, I got a bit nervous. Surely qualified technicians didn't hit planes with sledgehammers?

I assured myself that they would never let us take off in this broken-down jalopy. After three hours an excited pilot announced that the plane was fixed and that we would take off again. All the passengers on my side of the plane who had seen a small Thai man in flip-flops and a singlet hitting the plane with a sledgehammer looked around nervously! The plane taxied out of the hanger and made its way to the end of the runway, ready for air traffic control to give the okay for take off.

Moments later the plane lifted off and with each second that passed, gained more height. With each moment, I had growing confidence in the little Thai man in flip-flops and singlet top who had been hitting the plane with a sledgehammer.

The flight from Bangkok to London took approximately fourteen hours and ... oh yeah, did I mention that for that entire flight there was no air-conditioning, no in-flight entertainment AND the baby behind me decided to be sick on my seat? The combination of heat, sick and boredom made me want to ... kill ... some ... geese!

I have discovered that life is similar to flying in three ways:

▶ *1. A point of origin*
For that flight it was Bangkok. For your life it is your birth ... in fact, it is even before that (see Jeremiah 1:5).

▶ *2. A reason for flying*

For me on that flight the reason was that I was travelling to speak to some young people in churches. For your life, your "reason for flying" may be better defined as your *purpose*.

▶ *3. A point of disembarkation (the place you get off!)*

For me on that flight it was London and then onto Kiev. In your life the point of disembarkation is the moment you leave this life and go on to the next (eternity).

On my flight from Bangkok I remember thinking one thing: *"If I can just get through the next hour, then I will be closer to getting there."*

Similarly, on the day from hell that included, geese, paint, forgotten keys, more geese and ladders, I remember thinking, *"If I can just get through this next minute, then I am closer to getting through this nightmare of a situation."*

In 2002 a song hit the charts in England. Some of the words are:

> "If only I could get through this
> I just gotta get through this
> I just gotta get through this
> If only I could get through this."[1]

The Bible says a similar thing in Philippians 1:6 (emphasis added), *"being confident of **this**, **that** he who began a good work in you will carry it on to completion."* (Get ready for a play on words with THIS and THAT.)

If you can learn the very important lesson of getting through THIS (for example a nightmare flight or a day from hell or disappointment in a relationship, frustration at home or even the death of a loved one), then you can move on to THAT (for example, a new day, a new opportunity, a new season).

The trouble with many people is that in the middle of a THIS moment they bail out or do rash, impulsive things (see Next #5). If you can learn that your THIS will lead to a THAT, then you can make it through a difficult day, a tough season or a terrible moment.

If I knew what was going to happen next, I never would have got out of bed on the day of the paint can. But with each moment, I just had to get through THIS (ladders, geese, keys, white spirits) because I knew a THAT was coming (the end of the day!).

There are two things about THIS and THAT to help you fly well in life taken from Philippians 1:6.

1. Your THIS determines your THAT

Philippians 1:6 says, "... *being confident of **this**, **that** ...* "

In other words the THIS that you focus your life on determines the THAT – in other words, the outcome of your life.

- If your THIS in your thinking is small, your THAT will be smallness in life all around you.
- If your THIS in your heart is small, your THAT will be smallness all around you.
- If your THIS is that you are materialistic, your THAT will be that you will never have enough.

- If your THIS is one of worry, your THAT will be one of fear.
- If your THIS is that you strive, your THAT will be that you'll never fully enjoy life. Every moment you will be looking for the next thing, another way to break through, another way to move forward.

Turbulence

The first time I caught a plane I was two years old and I can't remember that, so let me tell you about the next time I caught a plane when I was fifteen. I was flying to England from Australia. As we flew over the equator I remember looking out of the window at some phenomenal thunder clouds. I began to watch an incredible lightning display. Dad said, "Glyn, God's putting on a fireworks display for you."

I soon realized that the storm that seemed a long way off was now a bit closer. Soon we were flying through the middle of the storm. I had never experienced turbulence before. The plane was shaking like crazy. I was sitting in fear. My THIS was that I was in un-chartered territory. I had never been here before. My THAT was that I was freaking out! Now, after nearly forty flights between England and Australia, whenever I hit a storm or some turbulence my THIS is that I've been here before. I know that turbulence is a normal part of flying. My THAT is, now I love turbulence because it takes away the boredom, the monotony of sitting in a hollow tube for twenty hours.

In life you are going to hit times of turbulence and whatever your THIS is will determine how you go through that turbulence. The Bible says that if I make my THIS, God, then my THAT will be good.

2. What's the track record?

Ask your THIS – the thing that you are focusing on, that consumes your mind – if you can have a look at its credentials.

The Bible says, *"being **confident** of this . . . "* The dictionary defines "confidence" as "to fully believe in something". You can only "fully believe" in something when you understand its credentials – when you know the thing you believe in has the power to back up your faith in it.

Imagine you are sitting on a plane. It's brand new, shiny, clean. It even smells new. The pilot comes on the speaker and says, "Ladies and gentleman, this is Cosmic Airways flight 937. You are now sitting on board the Z400 series airbus. It is the seventh one ever to have been built. Unfortunately, the other six crashed during their inaugural flights. This is the seventh and this is its first outing. Sit back and enjoy the flight!"

I've got a feeling that, knowing the credentials of this make of plane, you'll be sitting there a little nervous!

The pilot is fifteen!

When I was a youth pastor in Australia there was a kid in our youth group who, at the age of fifteen, had his pilot's licence. He could fly a plane before he could legally drive a car. I had seen him drive a car ... it wasn't encouraging! When he got his pilot's licence he said, "Glyn, will you come up in the plane with me? I need to get my hours up. I'll take you to 11,000 feet, we'll have a look around Sydney and then we'll come home." I said to him, "I am not getting in a plane with you!"

He was indignant. "Why?" he said. I replied, "Because I've seen you drive a car! And I'm not trusting myself with someone who confuses the brake and accelerator and thinks that the speed limit is a relative concept depending on whether or not their mum is around!"

When I fly, I want to know the pilot knows what he is doing. I want to make sure that he's got the right qualifications. If he has a degree in cooking I don't want him to fly the plane! I want to know that he's got his wings. I want to know that he's got a loving family at home waiting to see him. I want to know that he's not a daredevil, death-defying stunt man. I want to know that he hasn't got a heart problem or high blood pressure. What I want to do is make sure that the guy flying this thing knows what he is doing and that he has my best interests at heart! In other words, he has to have the right credentials and the right track record.

Perhaps you have allowed your THIS to be smallness or worry or fear or materialism or victim thinking or looking down on yourself or negativity or all these sorts of things? And this has meant that the THAT of your life has not been great! You've got to go back to your THIS and say, "Hey! Show me your credentials! Let me see your track record. If I'm gonna focus my life on you, you better tell me how focusing on you is gonna help me to live a better life!"

Ned Flanders and me

The Bible says, *"being confident of this, that he ... "* I'm not putting my confidence in a state of mind, an institution, or an ideology. My THIS, my focus for life, is found in a "He" and the "He" that the Bible is talking about is Jesus Christ. I know His track record; I know His credentials. The Bible says, *"In the beginning was the Word, and the Word was with God, and the Word was God"* (John 1:1) and *"God said, 'Let there be light,' and there was ... "* (Genesis 1:3). Colossians 1:15–20 tells us that everything was created by Jesus and for Jesus! Genesis 1 says that He looked at creation and He said it was "good", because the THIS of God always leads to the THAT of good.

My daughter came home from school the other day and said, "Daddy, do you know this song? 'He's got the whole world in His hands'?" I said, "Yeah Georgia, let me get the guitar." She said, "Daddy, how do you know this song?" I said "It's an old song. I used to sing it in Sunday school."

Some of her friends had come round and they said, "Wow! You play the guitar?" So, feeling like a rock star, we sat down to sing "He's got the whole world in his hands" and other songs like that. Then I thought to myself, "Oh no! I am Ned Flanders!"[2] So I quickly put the guitar away. BUT, He does have the whole world in His hands!

You see, Jesus' track record is that He is everywhere and every "when". Everywhere all at the same time and every "when" all at the same time because He's the Alpha and the Omega – He's at the beginning and He's at the end. He is in last month and He is in last year. That's why you don't need to keep going on about stuff that's happened in the past.

God's there now. He can fix it up. He can make you okay. He's also in your tomorrow which means tomorrow is okay. You don't need to fear! If your THIS is God and He's the focus of your life then you can know your THAT (your tomorrow) will be good.

Finishing off the sixth Next now – so I can get onto what happened next

Maybe your THIS is in the wrong place. Perhaps your THIS is looking at self, the obstacles in your life, your education and academic ability, dysfunctionality, gifts and talents, pressures that parents have put on you.

Perhaps it's time for you to say, "No longer will I be focused on THIS (whatever "this" may be). Because my THIS leads to THAT, and I don't want THAT to be the result of my THIS, I want a new THIS!

There was a time when my THIS was who my parents were. It meant that I was living a Christian life of pressure because my dad was a pastor and I had to be the pastor's kid. THIS led to THAT and at the age of twelve I had to make a decision that I didn't want my THIS to be based on other people's expectations of me any more. I just wanted my THIS to be based on my relationship with Jesus. That decision changed the THAT of my life dramatically. I grew in confidence that, *"He who began a good work ... will carry it on until the day of completion ... "*

That's why I know that if you make God your THIS He will complete a good work in your life – because God's vehicle is a vehicle of goodness. So I'm still confident that He who began a good work will carry it on until the day of completion. I'm still confident that I will see the goodness of God in my lifetime, because He is my THIS and THIS always leads to THAT!

Coming up:

"He was so fat that..."

Notes _____

1. "Gotta Get Thru This", written by Daniel Bedingfield, 2001, produced by Daniel Bedingfield and D & D Productions, mixed by D & D Productions.
2. He is on *The Simpsons*! Watch it some time.

Making it real for you!

1. What has been your THIS?

   ....
   ....
   ....
   ....

2. How has your THIS determined your THAT?

   ....
   ....
   ....
   ....

3. How do you think changing your THIS will change your life?

   ....
   ....
   ....
   ....

4. Take a few moments to pray and ask God to help you to change your THIS?

   ....
   ....
   ....
   ....
   ....

Someone once said,

**He who hesitates
is not only lost,
but miles from the next exit!**

Next #7

If I knew what happened next, I would...

...not have said sorry!

10:45am: After nearly an hour of scrubbing and cleaning we managed to get most of the paint off the pavement, floor, window frames, glass panes, parked cars, passing cars, low-flying ducks, shoes, spectacles, salon carpet, mirrors, scissors ... etc. But, the clothes of the men in the hairdressers were ruined. It was at that point that I did the heroic thing. I looked at all the irate customers who had stood around verbally abusing me for an hour, looked at them with eyes full of sorrow, seeking compassion, and said, "I am sorry I ruined your clothes!" Little did I know things were about to get worse!

The next day:

6:50am: Stopped and picked up Gaz at his house.

7:10am: Stopped at McDonalds and grabbed a hot chocolate and a hash brown

7:30am: Arrived at work.

7:33am: Got chased by the "guard geese" again.

7:34am: Drank a brew with Gaz and Pat, whilst plotting the demise of those geese.

7:45am: Smiled meekly as the guys re-enacted the previous day's events

7:58am: Got chased by the "guard geese" again. Pat laughed.

8:10am: Drank a brew with Gaz and Pat whilst plotting the demise of those geese. Began to wonder where the boss was...

8:22am: Boss arrived. I was scared to death. "This is the moment I get sacked from my first job!" I thought. I looked at him meekly. He smiled and then burst into laughter. Pat and Gaz started laughing uncontrollably. Even the geese seemed to enjoy the moment. It turned out that because I admitted guilt to the men whose clothes had been ruined, they were now suing us for creating stress in their lives and ruining their clothes. (To be honest, I felt like suing myself for stress-related fatigue.) The Boss said that because I did the heroic thing and apologised, that was all the ammunition they needed to sue the company. Why was I such a hero?

What heroes do

David is one of the greatest heroes in the Bible. He was only a teenager when someone prophesied that he would be the king; and he was only a teenager when he got the opportunity to fight the giant called Goliath. Read 1 Samuel 23:8–23. Those verses tell some fantastic stories about other great men (known as David's mighty men) who accomplished amazing things. There were two reasons that David's men could do those things:

1. Their leader (David) was a hero who had accomplished amazing things himself. They just followed his example.
2. They chose to be a part of David's crowd.

David's mighty men CHOSE to be part of David's crowd and we already know that we become like the people we hang around with. There are a few things we can learn from David's NOW to help us with our NEXT!

1. The Grab Factor

Read 1 Samuel 16:18. There was something extraordinary about David. Recently I went to see my football team play. After the game I went into the players' lounge for a coke. There were about thirty people talking and laughing, but when one of the players entered, everyone stopped and looked in awe.

It was the same with David. Whenever he entered the coffee bar (or whatever!), everyone looked in awe. As Christians we can have the same effect on people. People should be looking in awe at us. Not because of the Jesus' sandals and flowing robes, but because they recognize that there is something different about us. The fact that we live for Jesus should make a massive difference in our lives. It should be so attractive to people and so appealing that people want to know Jesus because of the way we live.[1] How does that happen? Read Acts 13:22!

David had a heart after God. The way for us to live lives that grab the attention of others is to "Have a heart after God and do everything He asks!" Life with Jesus is a life of fun, adventure and thrills – everything people are looking for. So then, how is your "Grab Factor"? Are people attracted to you because of God's presence in you?

2. Fight for the dream

Read 1 Samuel 16:1–13. Samuel prophesied that David would be the king. How's that for pressure? We talk a lot about destiny, but I like to think of it in terms of "God's dream" for our lives. Destiny is what God has dreamt we can be and do. Perhaps someone has prophesied over you (like David) that you would do amazing things? Maybe you were reading your Bible on your bed one night and God showed you some great things He wanted you to do in your life? The truth is that it won't just happen! You have to fight to make it come about! David was going to be the king, but before that, he had to fight Goliath. The fight against Goliath was more than just a little guy taking on a big guy. It was David fighting for the right to be the king. He was fighting to make a name for himself and he was defending God's honour. God's dream for your life won't automatically happen. You can't just sit back and hope it will happen – you have to fight to make it happen. What's the fight? Where is the battleground? The battleground is your everyday life and the fight so subtle that if the Devil can beat you here he has won! Your fight is a daily battle against being average, compromising, being complacent, settling down. You have to wake up every day prepared to make the most of that day. You have to fight the urge to turn on the TV or the games console and decide to have a chat with God instead. Why? Because you are determined to accomplish the dream.

3. It's all a matter of perspective!

Read 1 Samuel 17. Imagine how David felt on the day of battle. He would have been scared and in desperate need of a change of underwear! David was on the frontline and heard Goliath cursing God and the armies of God. But, while all the Israelites shook with fear, David said, "Who does he think he is? If you don't fight him, I will!"

All the people were saying, "He's so big, how can we kill him?" But David said, "He's so big, how can I miss?" Too often our perspective is wrong. Starting a lunch club at school may seem impossible; making a difference in college may seem too difficult; seeing people get saved looks too hard; but if we get God's perspective we'll say, "That's not too hard, because God will help!" In John 14:12 Jesus says we can do even greater things than He did. It's all a matter of perspective. Next time you think something is too hard, ask God for His view on the matter and you'll end up doing stuff everyone thought was impossible.

4. Stick a rock in its face

A teenager put a rock in the face of a giant! How could a boy do that? The answer is simple. David put his best into everything he did. Whether it was watching the sheep, fighting a lion or a bear, taking sandwiches to the frontline, playing the harp, or using his sling – he did it to the best of his ability. David must have practised for hours with his sling. The Bible doesn't say that an angel guided the rock to the giant, it simply says that David slung the stone and it killed Goliath. Who did it? David! Why? Because he practised and always did his best with whatever he was given. So often we classify things in order of importance and give our best to some things and not to other things. In order to do great things for God, we have to do our best in everything we do.

The Bible tells us that if we are faithful in small things, God will give us big things (Zechariah 4:10). David stuck a rock in the giant's face because he always did his best! There are a lot of giants in our land – immorality, substance abuse, the concept that church is boring, millions of people going to hell – all these are giants that God wants us to kill. If you do your best with everything you get to do, God will give you bigger things to do – and YOU could be the one who ends up sticking rocks in the face of giants in the nation.

5. Deal with second thoughts

Read 1 Samuel 17:48. Imagine the scene. David is on the battle line. He looks across at Goliath and says, "I can kill him!" From a distance, Goliath only looked two inches tall. But as David ran towards Goliath, Goliath was getting bigger. I am sure that at some point David must have thought, "What am I doing?"

Do you remember the first time you went on a roller coaster? At first you are tough, saying, "It'll be alright." But usually, when they strap you in and you start moving, you think, "What am I doing here?" David must have had to kill the thought that said, "What are you doing? Go back!" He had to keep going with the programme! Maybe you have noticed it's the same with us. At first when we start to do something for God, it seems great, but the more you do it, the more you begin to think, "What am I doing?" The Bible's advice to you is: DON'T STOP! DON'T GO BACK! (see Galatians 6:9). The next time you begin to do something that God asks you to do, don't stop. Don't entertain second thoughts. Don't go back and you'll kill another giant!

6. Becoming the hero that others follow

Read 1 Samuel 17:54. Before David fought Goliath he was simply taking some sandwiches to the frontline. Now, after killing the giant, he has his own tent! A bit weird? Maybe! Back in David's day the tent wasn't just something you slept in when you went camping in the summer, it was the place where you lived. It was a place of resource: you helped people, fed people, equipped people and trained people from your tent. David went from being a teenage shepherd boy to a hero that resourced other people. In other words, people were now beginning to look to him, following his advice and copying his example.

The truth about heroes

We all love a hero, but when you think about it, heroes are just people too! There are a few things about heroes you need to understand:

The heroes of faith

In Hebrews chapter 11 we read about the heroes of the faith:

- Abel offered a great sacrifice to God
- Enoch walked with God
- Noah saved mankind
- Abraham listened to God and left home for new nation
- Isaac brought blessing
- Jacob was given a new name (Israel) and a nation was named after him
- Joseph became prime minister
- Moses led people out of slavery
- Rahab saved the spies
- Gideon was a mighty warrior

The heroes of church history

In the second century AD a man called Tertullian defined two main theological concepts. He fought false teaching about Jesus, accurately stating that Jesus was both "fully God and fully man at the same time". He also created the term "Trinity" to help us understand that God is "three persons in one"!

In 1324, a man called John Wycliffe was born. He argued that it was wrong for the "common" person to have to rely on a priest for an understanding of what the Bible meant.

(At that time the Bible was only available in languages that most people could not understand, like Latin, Hebrew and Greek.) He made it his life's quest to transcribe and translate the Bible so that people could understand the Bible for themselves. He died in 1384. In 1428 the religious leaders of the day were so upset with what he had accomplished that they dug up his bones and burnt them at the stake! But because of Wycliffe you have the Bible next to your bed. He's a hero!

In 1519 Martin Luther had a revelation that we are saved by faith and not through good works. His life's devotion to this truth helped to fuel the Great Reformation in religious thinking, art and literature. What a hero!

Born in 1703, John Wesley preached approximately fifty thousand sermons. He wrote in excess of two hundred books. He trained over ten thousand preachers. He had over one hundred and thirty thousand followers and one third of Britain turned to Christ under his ministry. Historians tell us that it was largely due to Wesley that England didn't have a bloody revolution like France. He was a hero!

Two facts about heroes

1. Heroes are common people

The characters in Hebrews 11 are labelled as heroes, but in fact they were just common people.

- Abel was just a the farmer
- Enoch was a dad

- Noah was a drunk
- Abraham was a liar
- Isaac was nearly cooked alive
- Jacob was a deceiver
- Joseph had a few pride issues
- Moses was a murderer
- David was shepherd boy
- Rahab was a prostitute

And incidentally,

- Tertullian was so fat they had to cut away the table so his belly could slide underneath it!
- Wycliffe was born in Yorkshire (pretty common ☺)
- Luther was the son of a miner and he graduated thirtieth out of fifty-seven during his exams and suffered from depression.
- Wesley was the son of an alcoholic minister and he failed in his first efforts as a missionary to the Indians in North America.

None of these people were heroes so much as common people made good. If you are common, then you have the right credentials to be heroic!

2. They don't plan to be

The second thing about heroes is that they don't plan to be.

When David woke up and was sent to take sandwiches to his brothers on the battlefield, he probably didn't get up and say, "Today I will be a hero!" More probably he woke up and thought, "I have to remember those little lambs in the bottom field. If I don't move them into the top field today, they probably won't get the best grass!"

Tertullian probably didn't plan to invent a word ("Trinity") that would be used for ever, he just argued the case about Jesus and ate a lot of food!

Wycliffe didn't plan to be famous, he just fought for a cause he believed in. Luther probably didn't plan to be amazing, he just didn't want to be depressed any more. Wesley just didn't want to live as a failure! Enoch wanted to be close to God. Noah just did what God said. Abraham followed God's advice. Jacob was willing to change. Joseph dealt with his character. Moses was willing. David had a go. Rahab saw the opportunity to change. Gideon had nothing to lose!

Finishing off the seventh Next now – so I can finish the book

It's pretty simple really. Don't try to be a hero! Just learn to do what David did.

> *"When David had served God's purpose in his own*
> *generation, he fell asleep* [died] ... "   (Acts 13:36)

He served God's purposes and then he died!

David served God and Mike served the drunks ... sorry? ... you don't know about Mike? ... Here it is then ...

Mike was the son of a drunk! Mike also became a drunk and in his early teens was kicked out of home. He wandered the streets for years drinking anything and everything. As the years passed Mike damaged his brain and liver due to excessive alcohol intake.

One day he wandered into a city mission where he knew that if he sat through a preacher's sermon he could get a free cup of coffee and hot soup after the meeting.

For the first time during that church service Mike heard a clear presentation of the gospel and realized that he needed to get his life right with God by having a relationship with Jesus. Mike prayed and asked God to forgive him for the life he had led and accepted Jesus as his personal Saviour.

Mike broke his addiction to alcohol through the power of God at work in him, but because of the effects of alcohol on his body, he was still unemployable. Mike started to attend the city mission every day. He would pick drunk men out of the gutter, shower them and put them in clean clothes and into a clean bed in the mission centre. When drunks were sick on the front steps of the mission, Mike would clean it up. There was nothing that Mike wouldn't do to help people.

As the years passed Mike helped more and more people. One day a visiting preacher came to speak in the City Mission centre. When he asked the men in the room if any of them wanted to change, one man ran to the front, fell on his knees and started to cry, "Make me like Mike, make me like Mike ... " The wise preacher bent down and asked the man, "Don't you mean, 'Make me like Jesus?' " The man on the ground looked up through tear-stained eyes and said, "I don't know. Is Jesus like Mike?"

Now that's a hero!

Coming up:
"The END!"

Note

1. Read the second book in this series, *If I Had a Face Like Yours* –
   it is all about that!

Making it real for you!

1. On a scale of 1 to 10, how attractive do you make God look through the way you live? (Circle the answer)

   1 – 2 – 3 – 4 – 5 – 6 – 7 – 8 – 9 – 10
   (lowest)   (highest)

2. What does it mean to you to "fight for the dream?"

   ....

   ....

   ....

   ....

   ....

3. In what areas are you NOT doing your best?

   ....

   ....

   ....

   ....

   ....

4. Do you think you could become a hero that other people follow? Why or why not?

   ....

   ....

   ....

   ....

   ....

Someone once said,

"All those who believe in telekinesis, raise my hand."

The last bit!

Frustrating as it may seem, the fact that we don't know "what happens next" in life only adds to the adventure of each day. The genius of the day is that *you are never quite sure what is going to happen next!* You can't be sure, but there are several things you can do NOW to help your NEXT. If I knew what happened next, I would...

- ... not have gone to work that day (re-define your starting point)
- ... not have put that stick there (learn to think!)
- ... not have stopped to talk to that geezer (move from LONG TIME to SHORT TIME)
- ... have double-checked (remember that faith is also a position)
- ... not have rushed off with such haste (relax – "the Man" has a plan!)
- ... have checked the roof (remember, THIS leads to THAT)
- ... not have said sorry (faith is not for heroes)

The other day my friend sent me an email. It read,

> I want to live my next life backwards. You start out dead and get that out of the way. Then you

wake up in an old age home feeling better every day.

You get kicked out for being too healthy, go collect your pension, then, when you start work, you get a gold watch on your first day. You work until you're young enough to enjoy your retirement. You generally have lots of fun and then get ready for high school. You become a child, go to primary school, you play, you have no responsibilities, you become a baby and then ... you spend your last nine months floating peacefully in luxurious spa-like conditions with central heating, room service on tap, and with larger quarters every day.

Unfortunately we can't live our life backwards (in retrospect), we can only live our lives moving forwards. You'll never know what will happen next, but if you put the principles of this book into practice NOW, then my prayer is that your NEXT will be all you hope it is.

Live confident! You're a champion!

Coming up:

"If I was a hero!"

Someone once said,

"You are slower than a herd
of turtles stampeding through
peanut butter."

Further information

About the author

Glyn Barrett is the Senior Pastor of *Audacious City Church* in Manchester, England. He is also the director of *Youth Alive UK* and *Audacious*. He is a dynamic communicator and a sought-after speaker throughout the world. Glyn is married to Sophia. They have two children, Georgia and Jaedon.

Other books by Glyn Barrett

Glyn is the author of three books: *If I Was the Devil* (Sovereign World, 2004), *The Audacious Revolution* (New Wine Press, 2005) and *If I Had a Face Like Yours* (New Wine Press, 2006).

Contact details, information and resources

www.liveaudacious.com
www.audaciouscitychurch.com
www.youthaliveuk.com
Email: info@liveaudacious.com

We hope you enjoyed reading this New Wine book.
For details of other New Wine books and
a range of 2,000 titles from other
Word and Spirit publishers visit our website:
www.newwineministries.co.uk